calm
YOUR ANXIETY

Other Books by Robert J. Morgan

calm

YOUR ANXIETY

winning the fight against worry

ROBERT J. MORGAN

W PUBLISHING GROUP

AN IMPRINT OF THOMAS NELSON

Calm Your Anxiety

© 2023 Robert J. Morgan

Portions of this book were excerpted and adapted from *Worry Less, Live More.*

All rights reserved. No portion of this book may be reproduced, stored in a retrieval system, or transmitted in any form or by any means—electronic, mechanical, photocopy, recording, scanning, or other—except for brief quotations in critical reviews or articles, without the prior written permission of the publisher.

Published in Nashville, Tennessee, by W Publishing, an imprint of Thomas Nelson.

Published in association with Yates & Yates, www.yates2.com

Thomas Nelson titles may be purchased in bulk for educational, business, fund-raising, or sales promotional use. For information, please e-mail SpecialMarkets@ThomasNelson.com.

Unless otherwise noted, Scripture quotations are taken from the Holy Bible, New International Version®, NIV®. © 1973, 1978, 1984, 2011 by Biblica, Inc.® Used by permission of Zondervan. All rights reserved worldwide. The "NIV" and "New International Version" are trademarks registered in the United States Patent and Trademark Office by Biblica, Inc.®

Scripture quotations marked AMP are from the Amplified® Bible (AMP). © 2015 by The Lockman Foundation. Used by permission. www.Lockman.org

Scripture quotations marked GNT are from the Good News Translation in Today's English Version—Second Edition. Copyright © 1992 by American Bible Society. Used by permission.

Scripture quotations marked HCSB are from the Holman Christian Standard Bible®. © 1999, 2000, 2002, 2003, 2009 by Holman Bible Publishers. Used by permission. HCSB® is a federally registered trademark of Holman Bible Publishers.

Scripture quotations marked KJV are taken from the King James Version. Public domain.

Scripture quotations marked THE MESSAGE are from *The Message.* © 1993, 2002, 2018 by Eugene H. Peterson. Used by permission of NavPress. All rights reserved. Represented by Tyndale House Publishers, a Division of Tyndale House Ministries.

Scripture quotations marked NCV are from the New Century Version®. © 2005 by Thomas Nelson. Used by permission. All rights reserved.

Scripture quotations marked NKJV are from the New King James Version®. © 1982 by Thomas Nelson. Used by permission. All rights reserved.

Scripture quotations marked NLT are from the Holy Bible, New Living Translation. © 1996, 2004, 2015 by Tyndale House Foundation. Used by permission of Tyndale House Ministries, Carol Stream, Illinois 60188. All rights reserved.

Scripture quotations marked PHILLIPS are from The New Testament in Modern English by J. B. Phillips. © 1960, 1972 J. B. Phillips. Administered by the Archbishops' Council of the Church of England. Used by permission.

Scripture quotations marked THE VOICE are from The Voice®. © 2012 by Ecclesia Bible Society. Used by permission. All rights reserved. Note: Italics in quotations from The Voice are used to "indicate words not directly tied to the dynamic translation of the original language" but that "bring out the nuance of the original, assist in completing ideas, and . . . provide readers with information that would have been obvious to the original audience" (The Voice, preface).

Italics added to all other Scripture quotations represent the author's own emphasis.

Any internet addresses, phone numbers, or company or product information printed in this book are offered as a resource and are not intended in any way to be or to imply an endorsement by Thomas Nelson, nor does Thomas Nelson vouch for the existence, content, or services of these sites, phone numbers, companies, or products beyond the life of this book.

ISBN 978-1-4003-3430-8 (Paperback)
ISBN 978-1-4003-3551-0 (eBook)
ISBN 978-1-4003-3552-7 (Audio)

Library of Congress Control Number:

2023002233

Printed in the United States of America

23 24 25 26 27 LBC 5 4 3 2 1

Contents

You Too? Then We're in This Together!

Here's something you should know about me right up front: I'm a pastor who battles anxiety. I've battled anxiety ever since childhood, and I have a journal full of war stories to prove it.

Nothing grips my spirit like anxiety. It's a spider spinning webs in my mind, complicating my emotions, distracting my thoughts, raising my heart rate. And when life tightens the strings hard enough, I am sometimes drawn into fetal levels of fear despite having memorized virtually every verse in the Bible about worry and about peace.

I'm sorry to confess such a thing, but by nature and probably also nurture on my mother's side of the family, I am prone to stress reactions that wreak havoc with on nervous system. I remember my mom standing on the porch of our home in Elizabethton, Tennessee, wringing her hands when ambulances raced up highway 19-E in the direction of our apple orchard, twenty miles away.

Thousands of people lived up that road, but my mother always worried my dad had suffered an accident.

As a child, I anguished over misplaced library books, and my first panic attacks came when I had to give oral reports in school. It's tough to get through the social pressures of school, the insecurity of dating and courtship, and the changes required for marriage when you're too insecure to talk to people or risk rejection. One tends to burrow into one's own world. I like it here in my own world—but not if I'm padlocked in by anxiety.

However, I can't blame it all on DNA or my upbringing. It's also a byproduct of being human. Anxiety, which is essentially a strain of fear, is a common response to real pressures and problems. Anybody can experience life-interrupting moments of anxiety, but in our post-Covid world—a world vastly different from the world we knew prior to 2020—life seems harder than we ever expected it would be, and this has not only disrupted but destroyed many people's sense of well-being. Socially, economically, politically, relationally . . . nothing's the same as it was. The upheaval and loss and changes that we've all endured have been like a jackhammer, tearing away at our security layer by layer.

Even the Lord Jesus, the Prince of Peace Himself, didn't dismiss the difficulties of this life. "Each day has enough trouble of its own," He admitted (Matthew 6:34). "In this world you will have trouble," He said (John 16:33).

On one occasion, He even remarked, "Now my soul is troubled, and what shall I say?" (John 12:27).

If Jesus' soul could be troubled, your soul and mine are certainly in the crosshairs of the hurtful, hurting world we live in. The trials of this life seem to be getting worse. In more than forty years of pastoral counseling, I've seen a lot of cultural changes, but nothing like what's happened in the past few years. It seems to me we're at a flood stage of angst. Loneliness, isolation, grief, suicidal thoughts—they're not just somebody else's struggles anymore. They're *our* struggles, or those of someone we know and love. I see it and hear it among the people in my church and community, I feel it within myself, and I read about it in the headlines.

Anxiety disorders comprise the most common mental illness in America, affecting anywhere from 25 to 30 percent of adults. What's more, according to the World Health Organization,[1] the pandemic triggered a 25 percent increase in anxiety and depression worldwide. Whether or not you fall within that number—clinically speaking— like I do, there's no doubt that, humanly speaking, a full 100 percent of us worry about life every day. People are anxious and upset. We're overextended and running on empty. We're worried and we're weary. One moment we're alarmed about global politics or potential layoffs, and the next we're frustrated with a clogged commode or a negative comment online. Stress keeps us on pins and needles all day long and well into the night, and there's a strain over everything we do, even when we're having fun.

I'm writing these words on a balcony in Naples, Florida, overlooking the Gulf of Mexico. Below me are palm trees, sea gulls, a lovely pool, and a placid ocean with soft, rhythmic waves. Yet anxiety never takes a vacation. There's seldom a time when I feel totally free from inklings of fear, and even now I have a nagging feeling of foreboding about things back home.

The rich and famous are not immune either. When a successful actress was interviewed by *Glamour* magazine years ago, the reporter asked her why she was reclusive, why she didn't go out and have more fun. The young celebrity replied, "It's sad, actually, because my anxiety keeps me from enjoying things as much as I should at this age."

"Really?" said the journalist. "I know a lot of young women suffer from anxiety. It's brave of you to talk about it."

The starlet explained, "[I take] pills, long-term pills. . . . It makes me tired all the time. Anxiety, it just stops your life."[2]

Perhaps you also know from personal experience how anxiety in its many forms can stop or hinder your joy, stamina, enthusiasm, confidence, and wellness. Someone defined worry as a small trickle of fear that meanders through the mind and cuts a channel into which all other thoughts are drained.[3] Anxiety is that and more. It's a river of disquiet and dis-ease in our souls. Sometimes it's nothing more than a flutter or a knot in our stomachs; other times it manifests itself in panic attacks or posttraumatic stress episodes; often we're gripped by fistfuls of fear that overwhelm our circuits.

If at any point you've been reading and nodding your head saying, "Me too. I can relate!"—well, then, we're in this struggle together, comrades in a common war. Yet whatever our circumstances, whatever our genetic predispositions, whatever our personality or background, we are capable of pressing toward the goal of greater wholeness.

Professional counselors, therapists, doctors, and people with giftings of wisdom can help us tremendously. Nutrition, exercise, rest, and good habits make a big difference in how we handle stress. Prescribed medication, used wisely, can play a positive role. But medical treatment alone is incapable of reaching the hidden depths of the soul. We need help from beyond ourselves and from beyond our worried world. The German humanitarian George Müller spoke for many of us when he said, "Many times when I could have gone insane from worry, I was in peace because my soul believed the truth of [God's] promise."[4]

We must attack anxiety on the basis of spiritual truth. God expects—and equips!—us to fight this affliction with every available spiritual weapon, not just the therapeutic ones. Nothing can replace a spiritual foundation based on the Lord Jesus Christ. No self-improvement method can exceed having your spirit, soul, and body governed by the Holy Spirit. No therapy in the world can match the theology of the Bible or the healing in its words.

Time and again in my own life, the contemplation of Scripture has calmed and freed my mind better than the wisest counselor or the newest drug. But what has taken the comfort of God's Word to the next level in my life has been learning to make the promises and truths of Scripture a part of my regular routine.

I got this idea in large part from a man with whom I'm familiar—another struggler with anxiety. He was an energetic worker who left home to roam the globe as a spiritual ambassador, a missionary. Traveling to a picturesque corner of the Mediterranean, he came to a port on the Aegean Sea, beautiful in its setting, and famous for its grapes, wine production, and white cheese. Sailors, importers, exporters, students, and philosophers from across Europe and Asia flowed through the gates and harbors of this city. Fishermen and financiers were equally at home within its borders. Yet it was a dark place, a city badly needing hope, needing spiritual light, needing a church.

My friend, an experienced missionary strategist, was as dedicated as anyone you've seen. As he explored the neighborhoods of the city, his heart yearned within him, and he instinctively saw the possibilities of launching a meaningful ministry. The city was a virtual open door for humanitarian aid and evangelism.

But, alas, something stopped this man in his tracks, and he abruptly abandoned the work before it even started. The problem wasn't related to politics or finances or failing health. There were no issues with his visa. The man simply suffered an anxiety attack triggered by an event far away, and at the moment of greatest opportunity, his emotions were hijacked by a wave of desperation that robbed him of his ability to concentrate. He became so obsessed by his distress that he could not function. In a state of jittery panic, the man packed his bags and moved on like a vagabond, unable to focus, unable to pursue his work.

He later described what happened to him:

> Now when I went to Troas to preach the gospel of Christ
> and found that the Lord had opened a door for me, I still
> had no peace of mind, because I did not find my brother
> Titus there. So I said goodbye to them and went on to
> Macedonia. . . . When we came into Macedonia, we had
> no rest, but we were harassed at every turn—conflicts on
> the outside, fears within. (2 Corinthians 2:12–13; 7:5)

The missionary who suspended his work in Troas was the apostle Paul. He grew so worried about the problems in distant Corinth that he couldn't focus on the possibilities in Troas. Paul had expected Titus to meet him in Troas with updates and, he hoped, with better news. But

Titus never showed up, and Paul couldn't concentrate on the work at hand.

To me, this is a remarkable admission. It shows the human side of a great biblical hero. It indicates the apostle was high-strung, full of nervous energy, and predisposed toward anxiety. He battled "fears within" as acutely as he battled "conflicts on the outside." Just like you and me.

As the Bible reminds us, the missing pieces for most people in their personal arsenal are the peace of God and the God of peace. On the following pages, I want to lead you—as a pastor but, even more so, as a fellow pilgrim— through what God has to say about dealing with anxiety and opening yourself to His overwhelming peace.

Incidentally, if you've read any of my books, you know they're packed with Scripture because I believe that within its lines is where the electricity flows between heaven and earth, and between God and us. Psalm 119:130 says, "The unfolding of your words gives light." So not only will we focus on God's Word, but the study questions at the end of each chapter are designed to take you deeper, cultivating peace of mind and heart. All you need is an open Bible and a pencil.

In Philippians 4, the Lord used Paul himself to remind the faithful that it *is* possible to erase anxious thoughts and compose our minds with peace "in every situation" (v. 6). For that to happen, though, we must "put . . . into practice" (v. 9) certain biblical ideals.

The word *practice* implies we must go to work developing certain skills until we are proficient, like an athlete or musician, or until they become habitual. In her book *Better Than Before: What I Learned About Making and Breaking Habits*, Gretchen Rubin called habits "the invisible architecture of daily life. We repeat about 40 percent of our behavior almost daily, so our habits shape our existence, and our future."[5] She also added, "Our habits are our destiny. And changing our habits allows us to alter that destiny."[6]

As it related to his anxiety, it appears Paul made a lot of progress in changing his habits and destiny between the years AD 55 (when he wrote of his anxiety in 2 Corinthians) and AD 62 (when he wrote in Philippians of a peace that transcends understanding). We can do the same. We may never achieve total immunity from anxiety on earth. It may be impossible to avoid worrisome episodes in life, but Paul was determined to have "less anxiety" and to improve his mental health. He wanted to experience peace and calm. And through his words and example, as well as those of other biblical writers, we can pinpoint several perpetual habits—eight of which we will be exploring in this book— that contribute toward a gradual and glorious experience with the God of peace.

The Bible teaches us that we can make progress; we can move from fretfulness to faithfulness. So do the lives of fellow believers throughout history. In the following pages, I invite you to explore with me the truths and testimonies that have guided me to a wonderful discovery: while there are good reasons to be concerned in today's world, there are *better* reasons not to be. God doesn't want us to be weakened by worry but fortified by grace.

In one of the Bible's hallowed benedictions, we're given this simple blessing:

> Now may the Lord of peace himself give you peace at
> all times and in every way. The Lord be with all of you.
> (2 Thessalonians 3:16)

At all times and in every way, the Lord of peace Himself wants to give you peace. Keeping this close to heart, let's delve into the very words of God, determined to bring ourselves into a better place mentally, emotionally, and spiritually through some of the peace-giving, proactive habits that our Creator recommends.

It's time for us to wage war on our runaway emotions with the weapons provided in God's unfailing Word. By developing strong disciplines highlighted in Scripture, you can calm your anxiety and gain a greater sense of God's peace and presence in your day-to-day no matter what's happening in the world around you.

CHAPTER 1

The Habit of Joy

If I had a dollar for every time I've heard someone say, "I just want to be happy," I think I'd be a contender for the *Forbes* list of America's wealthiest people, right up there with the likes of Warren Buffett and Oprah. Especially if I include the number of times I've said or thought it myself! The Bible, however, mentions little about being happy, because *happiness* is an emotion that comes and goes depending on *happenings*. The Bible speaks of something deeper—*joy* and *rejoicing*—,which are dispositions of the heart. That's why joy and sorrow are not mutually exclusive. Jesus was anointed with the oil of joy, yet He wept (Hebrews 1:9; John 11:35). The apostle Paul spoke of being sorrowful, yet always rejoicing (2 Corinthians 6:10).

Happiness is an emotion; joy is an attitude. Attitudes are deeper. They are richer. And the right attitudes provide the soil for healthier emotions as we mature. Emotions come and go, but attitudes come and grow. According to the Bible, one step toward overcoming anxiety is cultivating the attitude of rejoicing.

It's not "don't worry, be happy" like Bobby McFerrin wrote in his hit song back in 1988. It's "Rejoice in the Lord," an Old Testament expression passed along among believers starting in the centuries before Christ's birth. Paul later added that we should rejoice "always" and not be anxious about anything (Philippians 4:4, 6).

It's possible for you to be joyful today. Calming your anxiety and waging war on worry begins with choosing to tap into the Lord Himself as the fountainhead of hope and as our reservoir of joy. But what does it actually mean to "rejoice in the Lord"? After considering this for many years, I've come to see it as not only a command we obey but a choice we make.

A COMMAND AND A CHOICE

I understand this as a command because the eleven Old Testament references to *"rejoice in the Lord"* convey as much authority as the Ten Commandments. Which means that when we read the words "Rejoice in the Lord," we can preface them with "Thou shalt . . ." This is something God expects. It's a part of obedience and righteousness, and neglecting it is a sin.

Let's quickly trace some of the very stressful situations where this phrase was used in the Old Testament.

- The first person to have uttered the words "Rejoice in the Lord" was Hannah, a woman who had battled extreme anxiety because of severe struggles in her home. But in 1 Samuel 2, the Lord bestowed grace amid her troubles, and, as she worshipped with her little boy, Samuel, in the tabernacle in Shiloh, she exclaimed, "My heart *rejoices in the Lord*" (v.1). She had found the secret of converting her pain into praise.

- The next time we see this phrase is from the pen of David, after he repented of devastating sin. He found God's forgiveness, brought himself back into the will of the Lord, and exclaimed in Psalm 32:11: "*Rejoice in the Lord* and be glad, you righteous; sing, all you who are upright in heart!"

- We also come across this phrase in Psalm 35, when David was fighting off an attack by his enemies. He prayed for deliverance and pledged to "*rejoice in the Lord* and delight in his salvation." He declared, "My whole being will exclaim, 'Who is like you, Lord? You rescue the poor from those too strong for them'" (vv. 9–10).

- Isaiah 29:19 reveals that those who had been brought low or were lacking resources in Israel would still find joy: "Once more the humble will *rejoice in the Lord*; the needy will rejoice in the Holy One of Israel."

- Joel 2:23 indicates that even the changing of the seasons is cause for rejoicing: "Be glad, people of Zion, *rejoice in the Lord* your God, for he has given you the autumn rains because he is faithful."

- At the end of the book of Habakkuk, we read a passage that represents the most visual depiction of raw faith in God's Word: "Though the fig tree does not bud and there are no grapes on the vines, though the olive crop fails and the fields produce no food, though there are no sheep in the pen and no cattle in the stalls, yet I will *rejoice in the Lord*, I will be joyful in God my Savior" (3:17–18). Even when everything else goes wrong, the Lord Himself stays upright, and we can rejoice in Him.

- The final Old Testament reference is in Zechariah 10:7, where the Lord promised that the beleaguered Israelites would see better days, be lighthearted, and instinctively obey the injunction to *rejoice in the Lord*.[1]

- According to Scripture, rejoicing isn't just a good idea, a pleasant suggestion, or a laudable quality. God's people are to enjoy life. God wants you to enjoy life. We ought to have joy, and it's not optional. It is a command from the God of all joy who doesn't want His children doubting His providence, distrusting His promises, or discounting His sovereignty.

- Rejoicing in the Lord is not only a command we obey; it's a choice we make. The Lord wants each of us to opt for joy. To choose it. But not in the way that motivational speakers and home decorators have popularized it. The biblical version of choosing joy doesn't turn a blind eye to our pain. In fact, there's nothing superficial about this decision.

- Rejoicing in the Lord demonstrates our willingness to trust God so much that our attitudes are affected. When we make up our minds to rely on Him day after day, in storm and sunshine, our burdens are lifted even if our circumstances for the moment are unchanged or deteriorating. Standing on His promises, our spirits are elevated and our emotions lift upward as our perspective shifts Godward.

Perhaps your spirits are low right now; mine often are. But it is unhelpful and even unholy to remain in such a condition.

Thankfully, God doesn't give us commandments without providing the grace needed to fulfill them. Like my brothers and sisters in Scripture, I've learned the hard way that I must exercise control over my own attitudes. More accurately, I must let the Holy Spirit have control over it. I don't have to live at the mercy of my feelings. I can choose to get up off the ground, to cast a heavenward glance, and to decide I'm going to serve the Lord with gladness. Frankly, that's difficult. I couldn't do it without the truth of Scripture and the grace of God. Yet there comes a time when we say, "I'm tired of living in fear when God has told me to walk by faith. He has commanded me to rejoice in Him always. I'm going to change my outlook to an uplook, even if I have to force myself."

During the coronavirus pandemic, I didn't worry much about catching it. I went about my business, wearing a mask when I had to. I gargled several times a day and sanitized my hands a lot. I was determined to carry on as normally as possible. But after I came down with the Omicron variant, I suffered months of fatigue. That's when I worried. *What's wrong with me? Have I gotten lazy? Why am I sleeping so much? Is this old age? Are my medications causing drowsiness? How can I be productive?*

It nearly took over my thoughts until I stood up on the inside and said, "Trusting God, I'm going to work when I can and rest when I must." Thankfully, the fatigue gradually wore off, and at least a small part of the victory was a change in my attitude.

We all battle discouragement. We struggle with anxiety. But with the power of Scripture and the indwelling of the Holy Spirit, we can learn to regulate our emotions. If I'm suddenly overcome with fear about my child's safety at school, I can pause, commit him or her to the Lord's keeping, and rejoice that the Lord is present with my child all the time. Perhaps we can't avoid being cast down, but we don't have to remain in that condition. We can say with the writer of Psalm 42, "Why, my soul, are you downcast? Why so disturbed within me? Put your hope in God" (v. 5). To choose to stay depressed or angry or anxious or fearful isn't an option we can afford. That only makes life harder than it already is.

The prepositional phrase—*in the Lord—is the key to both God's command and our choice.* We can't always rejoice in the state of the world or the status of our relationships. We can't delight in the people or problems that are plaguing us. Some days our job, our health prognosis, or our balance sheets look pretty grim. But whatever the circumstances, we can rejoice in our Lord.

- That means we rejoice in His *presence*, for in His presence is fullness of joy.
- We rejoice in His *precepts* and *promises*, for there is a God-given promise in the Bible to counteract every anxious thought or stressful spot in life. Psalm 19:8 says, "The precepts of the LORD are right, giving joy to the heart."
- We can rejoice in His *providence*, for we know that all things work together for good for those who love Him (Romans 8:28).

- We can rejoice in His *pardon*, for with His forgiveness comes restoration of His joy.
- We can rejoice in His *paths* and *purposes* for our lives.
- We can rejoice in His *provision*, for our God will supply all our needs (Philippians 4:19).
- We can rejoice in His *protection*, for He will never leave us or forsake us.
- We can rejoice in His *paradise*, for to live is Christ and to die is gain (Philippians 1:21).

In any and every situation, even when we can find few other reasons for happiness, we can choose to rejoice in our Lord, His attributes, and His infinite fellowship and grace.

A CONDITION WE CULTIVATE AND A CLIMATE WE CREATE

Joy should also be understood as a condition we cultivate during every season of our lives. The best way to generate joy in your life is to begin to nurture a relationship with Jesus and let Him transform your personality by renewing your thoughts (Romans 12:1–2; 1 Thessalonians 5:16–18). Just as we train a vine to form a topiary, we have to train our minds and our moods to follow the trellis of joy that is found in the Lord.

When I was a student at Columbia International University in South Carolina, the faculty and upperclassmen often told stories about one of CIU's graduates, Joy Ridderhof, the head of a missions organization known as Gospel Recordings, Inc. Joy wasn't necessarily joyful by temperament; she was a worrier. But her attitude began to change when she heard a sermon by Dr. Robert McQuilkin, who called worry a sin. He said it was "an offense against God as heinous as any crime man can commit."[2]

Joy decided to replace her penchant for worry with a routine of rejoicing, because that seemed a reasonable act of faith in light of the promises God had given in His Word. She decided on an experiment. Joy sought to deliberately and habitually trust and praise God for His willingness and ability to bring good out of everything—including her own mistakes. She adopted James 1:2 as her key verse: "Consider it pure joy, my brothers and sisters, whenever you face trials of many kinds."[3]

By a dogged study and application of Bible verses about rejoicing, Joy began to live up to her name and to change the very fabric of her personality. Throughout her life she dealt with loneliness, financial insecurity, ill health, difficult climates, exotic cultures, travel fatigue, and foreign governments, but she stubbornly met each difficulty with a determination to rejoice in the Lord.[4]

In my library, I have a small booklet written by her that tells of a period of time when, quite suddenly, Joy relapsed into worry and was overwhelmed with a burden of depression that seemed unbearable. "But from the start," she said, "I set my soul to praise the Lord even more than usual. I sang and rejoiced and the worse it became, the more I expressed praise and worship and thanksgiving to Christ. . . . I . . . knew God, through rejoicing, would be released to do mighty things in my life."

Day after day during this dark period, she chose to sing praises to the Lord, to spend time in thanksgiving, and to rejoice by faith. "As unannounced as it came," she said, "this battle ended and with it such an open door for faith that it seemed as though I could reach out and take the kingdoms for our Lord and Christ."[5]

I don't recall ever meeting Joy Ridderhof. I don't think I ever heard her speak in person. But even hearing others speak about her and her commitment to rejoice had an effect on me as a student. Perhaps it was because of her influence that one of the most popular hymns in our college chapel services was Charles Wesley's "Rejoice, the Lord Is King!"

Rejoice, the Lord is King,
Your Lord and King adore!
Rejoice, give thanks, and sing,
And triumph evermore.
Lift up your heart,
Lift up your voice!
Rejoice, again I say, rejoice![6]

As that hymn suggests, the joy of the Lord is not only

something to be cultivated, but it resets the climate of our souls, providing fresh air and warmer temperatures for ourselves and for those who share our environment. I'd rather be upbeat than beat up, and I don't want others to be beat up or cast down by my attitude. Attitude is the climate control setting for our marriage, home, school, workplace, or wherever we go.

We do have to work on acclimatizing ourselves in this way. For example, I've found it helpful to avoid artificial sadness. I no longer watch sad movies or listen to melancholy music. There is enough sadness in life without generating more of it.

Certainly there are times to weep and to mourn, and to grapple with heartbreak. But God does not want us to remain bogged down in such a state, nor does He want us to foster misery like the paid mourners at ancient funerals. The underlying attitude that serves as the bedrock of our emotions should be the joy of the Lord. We must learn to process our emotions in a way that allows us to continually cycle back to joy.

The Christians in Philippi were demoralized when they learned of Paul's imprisonment in Rome. I don't know if you've been to Italy in the summer, but the heat can be unbearable. In the winter it can dip below freezing. Paul was in an unheated and un–air-conditioned cell, in chains, facing a tense legal challenge for his freedom. He was older and unwell. He had hoped to be engaged in a fourth evangelistic mission; he dreamed of evangelizing Spain. Instead, iron chains rattled whenever he moved, and he had limited sanitation or sustenance. So it's no surprise that Paul's friends worried. They worried about his comfort and his safety. They were anxious about the future of Christianity. They were discouraged and fearful of persecution. But Paul's letter to them conveyed a positive tone. It created a climate of joy in their hearts.

We might think he'd be frustrated or depressed as he wrote to the Philippians. Somewhere in Paul's words, we would expect to hear a tone of self-pity, worry, or grievance. But, no! He considered his imprisonment to be something God allowed, and he had already seen some benefits from it. "And because of this I rejoice. Yes, and I will continue to rejoice" (1:18).

Isn't it amazing what God can do? But Paul didn't stop there. He told his friends, "Now I want you to know, brothers and sisters, that what has happened to me has actually served to advance the gospel. . . . Through your prayers and God's provision of the Spirit of Jesus Christ what has happened to me will turn out for my deliverance. . . . Whatever happens, conduct yourselves in a manner worthy of the gospel of Christ. . . . For I have learned to be content whatever the circumstances. . . . in any and every situation" (1:12, 19, 27; 4:11–12).

Paul's habit of rejoicing in the Lord had transformed him, supplying him with a steady attitude of optimism and peace. And his faith-filled joy spread through his contacts in prison, to the Philippians, and on to you and me through his writings. He practiced what he preached—rejoice in the Lord always!—and so can you, in any and every situation.

Katie Hoffman wrote an encouraging book entitled *A Life of Joy*, in which she described her efforts to teach herself to rejoice in the Lord even when things are far from perfect in her circumstances or home:

> From my own experience I know that it's hard to rejoice always, especially when my husband may not be doing what I want him to do. Though I feel like wanting to show him I'm upset by acting downcast, the Holy Spirit still reminds me to rejoice always. I've had to learn, sometimes on my face, that I need to rejoice always no matter what's happening to me or around me. I have had to learn that I can't ever let the actions of other people cause me to sin. I need to be holy before the Lord despite what any other person in all the world does. This is why I emphasize so often how necessary it is for us to keep our minds fixed on things above.
>
> And regardless of how angry or upset I may want to get at a situation, I still have to be filled with love, joy, peace, patience, kindness, goodness, gentleness, faith, and self-control (Galatians 5:22–23). I've also learned from experience that this can be almost impossible if I'm not set on glorifying the Lord Jesus at any and every cost.[7]

When we establish that climate, the sun of righteousness rises with healing in its rays, and the mornings bring fresh assurance of God's great faithfulness, mercy, and love. That bolsters our spirits and spans an enthusiastic life.

YOU CAN DO THINGS WITH ENTHUSIASM

I want to approach each day that way, don't you? We can! Rather than hesitating or feeling reluctant because we're worried, we can be excited about doing what God has given us to do.

One summer at the Word of Life bookstore in Schroon Lake, New York, I picked up a copy of Harry Bollback's memoirs, and I was hooked from the first page. Harry wrote of growing up in Brooklyn in the 1920s and '30s, and of joining the Marine Corps after graduating from high school in 1943. World War II raged, and Harry was sent to the Pacific. He described his first time in combat, which was on the tiny island of Peleliu. The morning before the battle, Harry found a quiet spot down in the hold of his ship and prayerfully read Psalm 91. As he read it, he came to believe God would preserve him through the war. That was an assurance he badly needed, for his experiences in the South Pacific were horrendous.

"In the battle of Peleliu, in my company of almost 200 men," he wrote, "I was one of only seven who got out without being killed or wounded." He told of his buddies being blown up, of body parts littering the ground around him, of near-death experiences, and of the trauma of war.

Returning home at the end of the conflict, Harry, who was a gifted musician, teamed up with an enthusiastic evangelist named Jack Wyrtzen. They drew thousands of people to huge rallies in New York's Times Square and Madison Square Garden. Wyrtzen was known for his broad smile, powerful preaching, and global vision—and for his ability to extend a gospel invitation that compelled people to come to Christ.

Together, Bollback and Wyrtzen cofounded a ministry called Word of Life. They established camping and conference centers around the world, beginning at beautiful Schroon Lake in Upstate New York. Young people streamed to Christ by the thousands at these centers, and the world's best Bible teachers traveled there to minister to vast crowds.

Harry and his wife, Millie, moved to Brazil to establish Word of Life ministries in South America, and Harry's adventures as a missionary in the Amazon rivaled his experiences as a marine in the South Pacific. He ventured by canoe into hostile areas where no man had ever returned from alive. Sometimes he dodged arrows; other times he was surrounded by naked tribesmen without knowing their intent. To make a long story short, Harry Bollback established churches in the jungle, camps in the cities, and left a trail of newly redeemed Christians wherever he went.

As I finished Harry's memoirs, I came away wanting to do more for the Lord than ever. My excitement was at a new level.

The next day, while speaking at a conference at Word of Life, I recommended the book to the audience, and immediately someone shouted out a whoop of joy. I later learned it was Harry himself, ninety-two years old, who, unknown to me, was in attendance.

The next day Harry invited me to his home, and I spent several hours with him and Millie. I asked him the one question that had perplexed me when reading his book. Near the end of his memoirs, Harry had written, "The one thing I do wish I could do all over again for the Lord, though, would be to have a little more enthusiasm than I had."[8]

"Harry," I said, "I've seldom read a story of so much energy, passion, adventure, and excitement as yours. Why did you wish you had lived with more enthusiasm?"

"Oh, Jack Wyrtzen!" he replied. "He was the one with enthusiasm! I wish I'd had enthusiasm like Jack's. He showed me that if you have *that*, you can do anything, you can get anything done. I wish I'd done everything with a little more enthusiasm!"

I'm with Harry. Looking back on my life, I wish I had done everything with more enthusiasm.

Enthusiasm is simply joy translated into daily life. When we rejoice in the Lord always, we're living with enthusiasm, and enthusiasm makes the difference.

The Bible says, "Whatever you do, do it enthusiastically, as something done for the Lord and not for men, knowing that you will receive the reward of an inheritance from the Lord. You serve the Lord Christ" (Colossians 3:23–24 HCSB). You and I can begin today! Start immediately by inscribing "Rejoice in the Lord!" on the walls of your mind. Repeat it often. Turn it into a song. Adopt it as a slogan—whatever will help you remember.

The joy of Jesus is essential if we're going to erase our anxious thoughts and experience God's irrepressible peace. Rejoicing is a command to obey, a choice to make, a quality to cultivate, and a climate to create for yourself and those around you. Practice this in all its dimensions until it becomes second nature. It's a spiritual habit that can begin to calm any anxious soul.

CHAPTER 2

The Habit of Dependence

In the realm of counseling and support groups, *dependence* is generally regarded as something to avoid. To be dependent on a substance, or on someone who enables us, takes us in the opposite direction of health and wholeness. In the realm of spiritual support for our souls, however, we do want to develop a lifelong habit of dependence—on God. Of relying on God. Of looking to God for peace, wisdom, and healing, especially through the practice of prayerThis was President William McKinley's way of life. McKinley was born into a devout Methodist home and born again at age fourteen at a Methodist camp meeting. According to his pastor, A. D. Morton, young McKinley stood up during a youth meeting and said, "I have sinned; I want to be a Christian . . . I give myself to the Savior who has done so much for me."[1]

McKinley's mother, a woman of intense devotion and prayer, taught him to pray by example and encouragement, but his greatest lessons in prayer were forged under the pressures of his duties as president of the United States.

One of his heaviest decisions arose in 1898 regarding the status of the Philippines after the Spanish-American War. One day, a delegation of Methodist leaders came to the White House, and McKinley told them how he had decided to resolve the crisis in the Philippines.

"The truth is, I didn't want the Philippines," he said. "I did not know what to do. . . . I sought counsel from all sides—Democrats as well as Republicans—but got little help. . . . I walked the floor of the White House night after night until midnight, and I am not ashamed to tell you, gentlemen, that I went down on my knees and prayed Almighty God for light and guidance more than one night. And one night late it came to me this way."

McKinley relayed the strategy that developed in his mind as he prayed: that the Philippines should be taken seriously and helped, that the United States should "by God's grace do the very best we could by them as our fellow-men for whom Christ died." McKinley added, "And then I went to bed, and went to sleep and slept soundly."[2]

Not only did prayer guide McKinley through his political career, but it was his first resort, his first response, to his very last earthly breath. As the president lay dying from an assassin's bullet in Buffalo, New York, in 1901, the Lord's Prayer was on his lips.

I love that little slice of presidential history because it illustrates what we should do when we don't know what to do, when our problems seem unsolvable, and when our burdens keep us awake at night. Human advice may help, but nothing compares to taking our burdens to the Lord and processing them through prayer, so as to arrive at guidance, wisdom, and peace.

Prayer is the buffer zone of the soul, where fear is repulsed and where grace and guidance are gained. This is the process described throughout Psalm 37: "Do not fret. . . . Trust in the LORD. . . . Take delight in the LORD. . . . Commit your way to the LORD. . . . Be still before the LORD and wait patiently for him; do not fret . . . do not fret—it only leads to evil" (vv. 1–8).

We read it in Christ's words in Matthew 6—"Pray to your Father, who is unseen . . . pray: 'Our Father in heaven.'" (vv. 6, 9)—and also in Philippians 4:6: "Do not be anxious about anything, but in every situation, by prayer and petition, . . . present your requests to God."

Eugene Peterson's freewheeling translation, *The Message*, states Philippians 4:6–7 like this: "Don't fret or worry. Instead of worrying, pray. Let petitions and praises shape your worries into prayers, letting God know your concerns. Before you know it, a sense of God's wholeness, everything coming together for good, will come and settle you down. It's wonderful what happens when Christ displaces worry at the center of your life."

In the Greek language of the New Testament, the word used for terms such as *anxious* and *worry* was often *merimnao*, which comes from a word meaning "to pull in different directions." Anxiety pulls your mind apart like a man being drawn and quartered. It rips and ruptures your thoughts and feelings. It makes you feel as though you're being torn in two.

What should do that to us? Nothing! Absolutely nothing! God's Word assures us from start to finish that *nothing* should agitate us, because *nothing* can separate us from the love of a God for whom *nothing* is impossible.

The better we grasp His boundless sovereignty, the less we'll worry about the everyday burdens of life. If we anchor our hearts in the bottomless depths of Christ's love, nothing can capsize us. When we truly claim the inexhaustible wealth of the Spirit's deposit, we'll be rich in the peace that transcends understanding.

DON'T LET YOURSELF BE PULLED IN DIFFERENT DIRECTIONS

If this advice to trust and pray instead of fretting were given only in these couple of places in the Bible, it would still be wonderful and welcomed, but it is *not* given only here. This word *merimnao* appears several other times in Scripture, and these occurrences consistently represent a divine inoculation against the pandemic of anxiety.

- *Merimnao* is found in the Greek version of the Old Testament (the Septuagint). In Psalm 55:22, the word is translated "cares": "Cast your *cares* on the LORD and he will sustain you; he will never let the righteous be shaken." The writer admits we have "cares," we have situations that tear at our minds, but he tells us what to do with them. Cast them upon the Lord, transferring them into His hands. Let Him handle the issues that threaten to destabilize us.

- In the Sermon on the Mount in Matthew 6:25–34, Jesus used the term *merimnao* (translated "worry") repeatedly, saying, "Therefore I tell you, do not *worry* about your life . . . And why do you *worry* . . . So do not *worry* . . . Therefore do not *worry* about tomorrow."

- In Matthew 10:19, Jesus told those being persecuted, "When they arrest you, do not *worry* about what to say or how to say it. At that time you will be given what to say."

- In Luke 10:41, the Lord used this word while gently upbraiding Martha, who had worked herself into an irritable frenzy. He said, "Martha, Martha . . . you are *worried* and upset about many things."

- In 1 Corinthians 7:32, Paul told the Christians to whom he was writing: "I would like you to be free from *concern*"—that is, from anxious concern, from *merimnao.*
- Peter used the word when he said, "Cast all your *anxiety* on him because he cares for you" (1 Peter 5:7). Notice the "all" in this verse. Nothing is too small for our Lord's concern or too large for His capacity.

How is it possible to obey commands and exhortations as counterintuitive as these? Fretting comes as naturally as breathing. Some of our earliest memories are the anxieties we encountered in childhood, and we seem to never outgrow our capacity to worry. I should know; I'm an expert on the subject.

Truthfully, I have a hard time accepting this biblical premise to depend on God rather than to be anxious. Anxiety is so deeply ingrained into my personality that I feel guilty when I *don't* worry. When something is deeply troubling me, I feel responsible to worry about it. There's a moral obligation, so it seems. How can I shrug off issues that so deeply affect me and those I love? If I don't worry, who will?

Well, that's the point.

As we turn our anxieties over to the Lord, He goes to work on them. He is able to guard what we have entrusted to Him (2 Timothy 1:12). God, being God, doesn't worry, but He does work. The psalmist said, "It is time for you to act, LORD" (Psalm 119:126). And God can do far more by His action than we can do by our anxiety. According to Ephesians 1:11, God has plans and purposes that work out everything—absolutely everything—in conformity with the purpose of His will.

FROM OUR HANDS TO HIS

But what exactly is the process by which we transfer our cares to God and tap into His peace for ourselves? There is only one way to do that: through prayer. Earnest, heartfelt, biblical prayer is the method by which we transfer our legitimate worries into the Lord's mighty hands, and by which He transfers His inexpressible peace into our fragile hearts.

Prayer is the closet where we change clothes and replace a spirit of despair with a garment of praise. It's the bank where we present the promissory notes of God's promises and withdraw endless deposits of grace. It's the transfer station where the pulse of fear is exchanged for the impulse of faith.

The verses that we've looked at don't describe a natural state, but a supernatural process. To stop being anxious and enjoy the transcendent power of God's peace requires serious commitment to prayer—to praying systematically, to praying methodically, to praying in faith, to praying in detail. The life of faith is a growing experience, and prayer is an ongoing process of abiding in our Father's presence, meeting with Him at every turn, consulting Him in every plight, and trusting Him with every trial. In prayer, we transfer our problems to the Lord, and He transfers His peace to us. That allows us to rid ourselves of the false guilt we sometimes feel when we stop worrying.

If we live long enough, perhaps we'll reach a level of maturity beyond all worrisome fear. I haven't reached that stage yet, but the Lord tells us in effect through Scripture: "When you find yourself ripped apart by worry, learn to use the power of My presence through prayer to unleash divine processes that can conquer worry, demolish strongholds, effect change, and inject powerful doses of transcendent peace into your hearts."

In every situation, our supernatural Lord wants to lighten our spirits and lift the clouds of uneasiness. Things are never as bad as they seem where He is concerned. All His resources are available through prayer, and none of His promises have expired. So stop worrying and start praying, taking time to especially note those items for which you can be thankful.

Our refusal to be anxious doesn't mean we aren't concerned, nor does it make us passive to circumstances. Concern is appropriate, and wise responses are needed, but anxiety is unhelpful. The zone between concern and anxiety is a slippery slope. I've often wondered how to know, at any given time, if I'm reasonably concerned or unreasonably alarmed. It's a difficult median, but here's the key: When our concern is healthy in nature, it doesn't debilitate us. When it begins to feel debilitating, it has morphed into anxiety, which becomes a vicious cycle. I don't know about you, but sometimes I worry myself sick over how anxious I am that I'm anxious.

When anxiety barges into our brains, it brings along a gang of accomplices—discouragement, fear, exhaustion, anguish, hopelessness, pain, obsession, distraction, foreboding, irritation, impatience—none of which are friends of the Holy Spirit. We have to throw those bums out of our hearts and minds. Prayer is how we open the door, shove them out, and let the peace of God rush in to secure our thoughts and feelings.

YOU CAN ALWAYS GO TO GOD

How often should we go to God? Always. We should depend on Him "in every situation," as Paul instructed (Philippians 4:6). Remember, he was writing his letter to the Christians at Philippi from jail, where he faced a host of discomforting conditions. Yet "whatever the circumstances," he continued, "I have learned the secret of being content in any and every situation" (vv. 11–12).

Many things were happening to Paul outside his control. But rather than living in anxiety, he had learned he could bring those circumstances to the Lord and pray about every one of them, knowing that under God's providential control each situation would, in the final analysis, turn in a good-ward and in a Godward direction. The Lord's providential ordering of all things for the good of His children is just as certain as the resurrection of Christ from the grave on the third day.

Sometimes we learn this on the fly. Awhile back, a New Zealand pilot named Owen Wilson wanted to do something special for his friend, Grant Stubbs, who was celebrating a birthday. Wilson offered to take his friend flying in a two-seat, micro-light plane. The pair took off after church one Sunday from the South Island town of Blenheim in the Marlborough region, flying northeast over the Golden Bay, around hills and over gorgeous landscapes and seascapes along the northern tip of the island. The weather was crystal clear and a panorama of splendor spread before them. But as they crossed a tall mountain, the engine sputtered and died. The plane began losing altitude, and at that point Wilson could see nothing but steep mountainsides descending into a treacherous sea.

Both men were Christians, and they prayed instantly and earnestly. Stubbs, who had grown up in a minister's home and been involved in Youth for Christ, prayed aloud as Wilson manhandled the controls. When it appeared the two would fly into a mountain, Stubbs cried: "Lord, please help us get over that steep ledge!"

They skimmed just above the ridge, and Grant began praying, "Lord, we need to find somewhere to land!" Just when all hope seemed gone, the men saw a small strip of land nearly hidden between two ridges. Wilson steered the plane in that direction. They glided into the narrow valley and touched down, bouncing to a stop. "Thank You, Lord!" they shouted.

Then they looked up, and just in front of them was a huge twenty-foot sign that said Jesus is Lord!

As it turned out, the field belonged to a Christian retreat center, which explained the billboard. The owners, who ran out to greet their unexpected guests, told them the field was usually full of livestock, but on this day all the animals were standing along the edge of the field, as though giving them room to land.[3]

Many times we fly into anxious situations in life. Our engines stall. We encounter turbulence. Perhaps we're bracing for a crash and things seem hopeless. But in every situation we practice the power of prayer, and that's how we discover the incredible truth that Jesus is Lord.

MAKING YOUR REQUESTS KNOWN

Sometimes the Bible speaks of *prayers* and sometimes it speaks of *petitions*. In the book of Ezra, we read of a dilemma the prophet found himself in: I [Ezra] was ashamed to ask the king for soldiers and horsemen to protect us from enemies on the road, because we had told the king, "The gracious hand of our God is on everyone who looks to him, but his great anger is against all who forsake him." So we fasted and *petitioned* our God about this, and he answered our prayer. (8:22–23)

In Jeremiah 36, the prophet Jeremiah gave Baruch these instructions:

> "Go to the house of the LORD on a day of fasting and read to the people from the scroll the words of the LORD that you wrote as I dictated. Read them to all the people of Judah who come in from their towns. Perhaps they will bring their *petition* before the LORD and will each turn from their wicked ways, for the anger and wrath pronounced against this people by the LORD are great." (vv. 6–7)

And the writer of Hebrews records that "during the days of Jesus' life on earth, he offered up prayers and petitions with fervent cries and tears to the one who could save him from death" (5:7).

What's the difference between these terms? Prayer is a general word for all our communication with God. *Petition* is more specific, referring to asking God for help regarding certain needs. Though I've only given you a few scriptural examples here, you can see that petitions are offered up in emotionally charged situations. They are never over something routine.

The way I think of the difference between the words is this: It's one thing to chat with a friend; it's another to ask him for a favor. Prayers are the consistent conversations. Petitions are the special circumstances—those times when we're calling in for additional support, direction, or help. Underlying it all is the biblical charge to take everything to God in prayer.

To state this anxiety-busting habit in another way, we should pray, pray some more, and keep on praying—leaving the line of communication wide open between heaven and earth.

None of us does this perfectly, but we can improve, we can learn, and we can grow in prevailing prayer. One of the keys is the diversification of our methods. When I'm in the midst of an anxious episode, I often find myself at a desk with my journal and an open Bible, asking God to stabilize not just the situation but me as well. I write out my fears and emotions, because stating them makes them more manageable. Then I search the Scripture to find verses that comfort my heart, and I write those down too. Then I pray aloud, sometimes writing out my prayers, sometimes pacing the room, kneeling, falling on my face, or going for a prayer walk, as I plead for God's help. Other times I'll seek out someone to pray with—my wife, my prayer partner, or a close friend.

Prayer can be practiced in countless ways. It's not just a matter of bowing our heads, folding our hands, and closing our eyes. In fact, when I went through the Bible studying the physical postures employed by biblical characters when they prayed, I was astounded to find no example—not a single one—of anyone in the Bible actually closing their eyes or bowing their heads or folding their hands in prayer. There's nothing wrong with such practices, of course, but the heroes of Scripture more often opened their eyes, lifted their arms, and looked upward when they sought the Lord.

They prayed:

- kneeling, sitting, lying down, falling prostrate, standing up, walking.
- under the canopy of the sky, in their rooms, in their closets, on the rooftops, in the caves, and in the belly of the whale.
- silently and aloud; privately and corporately.
- with sighs, spoken words, shouts, and songs.
- with tears and with laughter.
- in desperation and in delight.

They wrote out their prayers. They prayed long prayers and short ones. They prayed coming and going, at home and abroad, day and night. The Bible acknowledges the diversity of prayer methods when we're told to "pray in the Spirit on all occasions with all kinds of prayers and requests. With this in mind, be alert and always keep on praying" (Ephesians 6:18).

Sometimes our prayers continue over a long period of time. Daniel and Nehemiah each fasted and prayed for many weeks over certain matters. On the other hand, the publican in Luke 18:13 simply beat his fist against his chest and said seven words, "God, have mercy on me, a sinner."

Occasionally I'll find a phrase from Scripture to think about repetitively whenever fear or panic rises. A good example is Matthew 6:10, which says, "Your will be done, on earth as it is in heaven." That's a plea from the lips of Jesus that helps me know what to pray when other words fail: "Lord, Your will be done in this situation, as it's done in heaven." We can sense the poignancy of this phrase because at the end of His earthly life, in the garden of Gethsemane, our Lord circled back to it, saying to His Father in heaven, "May your will be done" (Matthew 26:42).

Finding phrases in the Bible is a powerful method of prayer. An acquaintance of mine who faced a terminal illness said he became too weak to pray very long at once, but a few words of Scripture would come to his mind, and he turned those into prayers that he offered throughout the day. From his years of Bible study and Scripture memory, he had an endless supply of materials to fuel the lamplight of his flickering prayers in the evening of life.

When we use the words of Scripture in prayer, we're praying as God would have us pray. The Bible is an immense prayer book, filled with verses that can be turned into prayers as easily as substituting someone's name for the original wording. For example, if you're worried about a struggling child or family member, consider Colossians 4:12: "Epaphras, who is one of you and a servant of Christ Jesus, sends greetings. He is always wrestling in prayer for you, that you may stand firm in all the will of God, mature and fully assured."

We can adapt this verse into a prayer for our loved ones: "Lord, I am wrestling in prayer for them, that they may stand firm in all Your will, mature and fully assured."

Having found a prayer that meets your need, it's important to offer it with the element of faith. We may not always have a great faith, but we can always have faith in a great God and in His unfailing promises. The Lord expects our trust, and it's insulting when we doubt the very words Christ died to confirm.

Prayer shouldn't be a hamster wheel of worry; it should be a launchpad of faith. We take our burdens to the Lord and leave them there. The book of James tells us to pray whenever we're in trouble, for the prayer of faith can make the difference. "The prayer of a righteous person is powerful and effective" (5:16). We can do this whenever the tide of anxiety rises in our hearts.

I've also found it helpful to think of prayer in three distinct forms.

EVERYDAY PRAYER

The most vital for me is everyday prayer. We must pray regularly, systematically, methodically, and daily. The prophet Daniel was so habitual in prayer that even his enemies knew his routine. Daniel knelt and prayed in the morning before going into his daily work; he came home and prayed during his midday break; and he prayed in the evening before going to bed (Daniel 6:10).

When I was nineteen, I had mentors who impressed on me the importance of beginning my day with morning devotions, and this habit has kept me afloat for more than fifty years. I discuss my own procedures in my book *Mastering Life Before It's Too Late*, but here's the short form: After arising and showering in the morning, I sit down at a small desk where I briefly jot down a few lines in my journal, read God's Word, work on some verse or another that I'm memorizing, and open up my prayer lists, thanking God for His blessings and asking for His intervention in things concerning me. I often pray aloud. Before leaving the spot, I consult my calendar and jot out a proposed agenda for the day. Psalm 143:8 says, "Let the morning bring me word of your unfailing love, for I have put my trust in you. Show me the way I should go, for to you I entrust my life."

It's as simple as that, but nothing goes right about my day if I neglect the practice.

Perhaps the morning hour doesn't fit your schedule. It's not a matter of having a time of *morning* prayer but of *daily* prayer, whenever works best. The things that mean most to us are the things we do daily. That's the glue of life that holds everything together. Jesus told us to go into our inner rooms and shut the door and talk to our heavenly Father in secret (Matthew 6:6). This implies a definite time and place for meeting privately with God in a way that allows us to realize and recognize His presence, drawing near to Him in dependence.

Some people keep a prayer list on the flyleaf of their Bibles. Others simply keep a mental list. My friend Don Wyrtzen told me how, over the years, he's developed a mental template that guides his prayers.

1. He begins his prayer time with an emphasis on the spiritual aspects of his life—praising God for who He is, what He does, knowing Him, loving Him, and trusting Him.
2. Don then moves to the relational aspects of his life, praying for himself, his wife, his children and grandchildren, his siblings, his extended family and friends, and those who need the Lord.
3. Finally, he prays about the vocational aspects of his life, his calling and work, his finances and opportunities.

When he prays for friends across the country, Don told me, he often moves from east to west, starting in Maine and praying for friends across America, ending in Southern California.[4] You could easily "go global" with this, praying around the world depending on where people are located. Prayer is extraordinarily adaptive to all situations so long as we practice it every day.

If this is a new habit for you, please persevere with it. When I mentor young adults in their prayer habits, I ask them to make unbreakable commitments for a period of time, with accountability measures in place. Learning to pray takes determination, but it's worth it. It can save you from a fretful, anxious life.

THROUGH-THE-DAY PRAYERS

There's another kind of prayer that helps us in every situation: through-the-day prayers. The Bible tells us to pray "continually," or some versions translate it "without ceasing" (1 Thessalonians 5:17). Prayer is a regularly recurring activity, not just from day to day but during each day.

In *Lessons from My Parents*, Stephanie Porter recalled a time when she and her brothers were putting on their snow gear to play outside, sledding and building igloos. But their mother stopped them. She had lost her wedding ring and was frantically looking for it. She asked the children to kneel and pray with her. They did so, and as soon as the "Amen" was finished, they jumped up to resume dressing. "My five-year-old bother slipped a foot into his snow boot and immediately pulled it back off," Stephanie wrote. "He turned the boot upside down and out slipped my mom's wedding ring. . . . We momentarily forgot about the snow and ran excitedly to show our mom that our prayer worked."[5]

The memory of that impromptu prayer stayed with Stephanie, and it has transcended generations. Stephanie wrote: "Now that I have my own kids, I teach them about faith. We pray every day before school, meals, and bedtime. . . . I hope my daughters will learn faith from me, as I learned it from my mother."[6]

When the biblical hero Nehemiah heard of the dilapidated condition of Israel's security, he sat down and wept and mourned and prayed for several days, finally composing his words into a written prayer, which is recorded in Nehemiah 1. In the next chapter, King Artaxerxes asked Nehemiah what was wrong and what he needed. Nehemiah 2:4–5 is very instructive: "The king said to me, 'What is it you want?' Then I prayed to the God of heaven, and I answered the king."

I wonder if Artaxerxes noticed the slight pause that preceded Nehemiah's answer. Before speaking to the earthly king before him, Nehemiah sent up a silent plea to the heavenly King above him—and his request was granted.

I have a friend who keeps a perpetual prayer list on a sheet of paper carefully folded in his pocket. It's always there, which allows him to pray whenever and wherever he is. He can't keep up with a notebook or journal, but he's never without his prayer list. When waiting to board a plane or stopped at a red light, he can glance down at his list and begin praying where he left off, and in this way he prays periodically from daybreak to bedtime.

Even without a list, we can learn to mutter prayers all day long, talking to the Lord as naturally as to a companion who never leaves our side. When prayer and quoting Scripture becomes as natural as saying our names or greeting a friend, we'll be on our way to spiritual maturity and transcendent peace.

D-DAY PRAYER

In crisis times, we may need to practice what I call D-Day prayer. Multitudes thronged Washington's Union Station on the morning of June 6, 1944, coming and going on their respective trains. For weeks, there had been rumors of an impending D-Day, when Allied Forces would invade Europe to turn the tide of World War II. On this morning, something incredible happened. No announcement was made from the loudspeakers, and there were no radios or newsboys shouting the message. But suddenly everyone just stopped. Conversations ceased. The invasion had begun, and news passed in whispers that American boys were storming the beaches in Normandy.

A beam of sunlight pierced the room like a cathedral. Suddenly a woman dropped to her knees and folded her hands. Near her a man knelt. Then another, then another, until all throughout the station, people knelt in silent prayer beside the hard wooden benches. A great railroad station in our nation's capital had become a palace of prayer.

Then slowly the woman rose to her feet. The man beside her rose, too, and within seconds Union Station was alive with motion and sound again. Across America, people paused to pray. The New York Stock Exchange opened the day with a time for prayer. The *New York Daily News* ran the Lord's Prayer on its front page. Prayer rallies gathered across the United States.[7]

That night, President Franklin Roosevelt went on the radio to address the nation, and he gave arguably the most moving speech in American history. I've seen the original draft in FDR's Presidential Library, and I still get choked up when I read it or hear a recording of the broadcast:

> My fellow Americans, last night, when I spoke with you about the fall of Rome, I knew at that moment that troops of the United States and our Allies were crossing the Channel in another and greater operation. It has come to pass with success thus far. And so, in this poignant hour, I ask you to join with me in prayer: Almighty God,

Our sons, pride of our nation, this day have set upon a mighty endeavor, a struggle to preserve our Republic, our religion, and our civilization, and to set free a suffering humanity. Lead them straight and true; give strength to their arms, stoutness to their hearts, steadfastness in their faith. They will need Thy blessings.[8]

After praying for the men in the armed forces, Roosevelt went on to pray for those back home—fathers, mothers, children, wives, sisters, and brothers. He ended his prayer with the words of the Lord Jesus: *Thy will be done, almighty God. Amen.* FDR's entire speech was nothing but prayer, but nothing was more needed at that moment in our nation's history.

From time to time, each of us faces our own individual D-Days, when we encounter difficult decisions, distresses, disasters, disappointments, or discouragements. Burdens press against us, foes oppress us, storms batter us. But no burden, foe, or storm can threaten the throne of God, which is why we come boldly to the throne of grace where we obtain mercy and find grace to help in time of need (Hebrews 4:16).

On every occasion. In every situation. Wherever we are—a train station, an airplane seat, a hospital bed, a courtroom, a cell, the cab of your truck, or the closet of your bedroom—wherever we are can become a cathedral of prayer and praise.

In the book of 1 Samuel, a woman named Hannah

had terrible family problems. She went to the tabernacle at Shiloh, and "in her deep anguish Hannah prayed to the LORD, weeping bitterly. . . . Hannah was praying in her heart, and her lips were moving but her voice was not heard. . . . [She said,] 'I was pouring out my soul to the LORD' (1:10, 13, 15). After Hannah gave her burden to the Lord, "she went her way and ate something, and her face was no longer downcast" (v. 18).

God had not yet answered her prayer, but she had turned her worry list into a prayer list, cast her burden on the Lord, claimed His victory, and changed her attitude accordingly.

We see this pattern repeatedly in the Bible.

- Abraham and Sarah prayed in their barrenness.
- Jacob pleaded for his sons.
- Moses prayed for water from the rock.
- Joshua prayed for victory in battle.
- Gideon prayed while hiding from the Midianites.
- David prayed while running from the armies of Saul.
- Hezekiah prayed during the Assyrian invasion.
- Jeremiah prayed as his culture collapsed around him.
- Daniel prayed for insights about the last days.
- Nehemiah prayed while building the walls around Jerusalem.

- Jesus prayed on the eve of Calvary.
- The early church prayed for boldness amid persecution.
- The apostles prayed for power from on high.
- John prayed when exiled to the island of Patmos.

In times of great crisis, we must pray and trust God with burdens heavier than we can bear. This isn't a happy-go-lucky affair. It's spiritual warfare, for, as Cameron Thompson wrote, "there comes a time, in spite of our soft, modern ways, when we must be desperate in prayer, when we must wrestle, when we must be outspoken, shameless, and importunate . . . plowing through principalities and powers, inviting His almighty power into our desperate needs."[9]

Despite the intensity of these special times of prayer, the process is remarkably simple. Hymnist Charles A. Tindley once counseled a man who was a chronic worrier. After listening to him awhile, Tindley advised him to take his burdens to the Lord and leave them there; as Tindley later pondered the advice he gave, he turned it into a beloved gospel song.

If the world from you withhold of its silver and its gold,
And you have to get along on meager fare,
Just remember, in His Word, how He feeds the little bird;
Take your burden to the Lord and leave it there.[10]

The benefits of depending on God sometimes come over us like a metamorphosis. This once happened to E. Stanley Jones. Though he had gone to India as a missionary with visionary passion, his energy had evaporated amid unbearable heat, hostility, and anxiety. He collapsed, and even prolonged rest failed to restore him. His nerves were shot. He resembled the apostle Paul at Troas.

One night in the city of Lucknow, while praying, Jones suddenly felt the Lord speaking to him. Though not audible, the Lord's voice almost seemed so. Jones sensed these words: *Are you yourself ready for this work to which I have called you?*

"No, Lord, I am done for," Jones replied. "I have reached the end of my resources."

The Lord seemed to reply, *If you will turn that over to Me and not worry about it, I will take care of it.*

"Lord," Jones said, "I close the bargain right here." At that moment a great peace settled into his heart and pervaded his whole being:

I knew it was done! Life—Abundant Life—had taken possession of me. I was so lifted up that I scarcely touched the road as I quietly walked home that night. Every inch was holy ground. For days after that I hardly knew I had a body. I went through the days, working far into the night, and came down to bedtime wondering why in the world I should ever go to bed at all, for there was not the slightest trace of tiredness of any kind. I seemed possessed by life and peace and rest—by Christ Himself.[11]

Jones labored on for decades, serving more than forty years in India, preaching around the world—sometimes three times a day—writing a dozen books, and becoming one of the most famous missionaries of his generation. From his evening encounter with the Lord at Lucknow until his death in January 1973, E. Stanley Jones lived in the glow of the sufficiency of Christ Himself, never forgetting the Lord's promise, "If you turn that over to Me and not worry about it, I will take care of it."[12]

The Greek philosopher Archimedes said, "Give me a lever and a place to stand, and I'll move the world." He was referring to one of the world's simplest machines, the lever, in which a long beam placed against a fulcrum can move large objects. The habit of depending on God, especially through prayer, is our leverage throughout life. Our prayers can move heaven and earth, for the prayers of righteous people are powerful and effective.

The world offers no better antidote to our cares and concerns than "Let the Lord handle it." We can give everything to God in prayer.

CHAPTER 3

The Habit of Nearness

We can more easily develop a calming, continuing dependence on God by regularly remembering how near He is. How present He is.

During my college days, a few buddies and I were hiking somewhere in a beautiful gorge when we detoured over a ravine by walking across a fallen tree. I was halfway across the thing when I froze up and got tottery. The ground seemed as if it were a mile below me. I recall flailing my arms like a windmill and shouting, "I've lost my nerve!" The friend in front of me instantly reached out and took hold of my hand. I could have pulled us both off the log, but somehow the momentary touch of my friend's hand gave stability. I regained my balance and made it safely to the other side.

I've thought of that many times when I've gotten

weak-kneed over other chasms, and it's the touch of a Friend's hand that has steadied me. The same is true for the heroes of Scripture. When Peter sank in alarm trying to walk across the choppy waters of Galilee, Jesus immediately reached out His hand and caught him, saying, "You of little faith . . . why did you doubt?" (Matthew 14:31).

Many of the Psalms speak of the nearness of God's hand:

- "I keep my eyes always on the LORD. With him at my right hand, I will not be shaken" (Psalm 16:8).
- "Your right hand sustains me" (Psalm 18:35).
- "I cling to you; your right hand upholds me" (Psalm 63:8).
- "Your hand is strong" (Psalm 89:13).
- "You will fill me with joy in your presence, with eternal pleasures at your right hand" (Psalm 16:11).

One of my favorite promises in Scripture—I found and memorized this verse in childhood—says: "Do not fear, for I am with you; do not be dismayed, for I am your God. I will strengthen you and help you; I will uphold you with my righteous right hand (Isaiah 41:10).

When you spot a couple walking down the street hand-in-hand, you know they're in love. The same is true for us in our love for Jesus. We enjoy the Lord's fellowship when holding His unchanging hand, and as we cultivate a sense of His nearness, we grow increasingly intimate with Him. We're strengthened and steadied by His presence.

The stresses of life rattle our minds. We feel tottery and worry about falling off the log. As we've seen, this even happened to Paul in Troas when he couldn't complete his mission. But the apostle worked through these issues, and we get a tiny but essential clue as to how he did in Philippians 4.

I have my Bible open there as I'm writing this, and one brief sentence has my attention. Just before Paul said, "Do not be anxious about anything" (v. 6), he offered this assurance: "The Lord is near" (v. 5).

Oh, how vital are those four words! *The Lord is near.*

Yet this is a difficult sentence to interpret. What did Paul mean by saying the Lord is near? That question has perplexed translators and commentators for two thousand years. Was Paul referring to space or to time or to both? If the first, Paul meant, "The Lord's presence is near." If the second, he meant, "The Lord's coming is near." If both, he meant, "Jesus is near, and that's true in two ways. He is near you presently, and His coming isn't far away either."

This dilemma is reflected in the various translations we use. Compare these two renderings from popular versions of the Bible:

- The Lord is ever present with us (THE VOICE).
- The Lord is coming soon (NLT).

Since Paul was a literary and theological genius who knew when a phrase could have a double meaning, and since both interpretations reflect unquestioned scriptural truth, I'm going to assume Paul meant: "The Lord is near to us—period—both in terms of His coming and in terms of His presence, so do not be anxious about anything."

Let me show you how this works out.

THE LORD'S PRESENCE IS NEAR

One application of the phrase "The Lord is near" in Philippians 4:5 has to do with

physical proximity. The Lord is close beside you right now, so don't worry; instead, pray. Almighty God is here, in our geographical zone, closer than we realize, now, accompanying us, surrounding us, sharing our space, even living within us. He is "an ever-present help in trouble" (Psalm 46:1) and close to "all who call on him in truth" (Psalm 145:18).

It's plain to see how this reality would lessen our quotient of worry. When we consider the nearness of Christ, we're reminded that He walks beside us every moment. He notices the look in our eyes, the tone in our voice, the catch in our heart, and the sigh on our lips. And He longs for His very presence to calm and control us.

Paul learned this from experience in Acts 21–23, when he encountered a series of disastrous events. After inadvertently sparking a riot in the Jewish temple, he was nearly killed by a mob, only to be rescued by Roman soldiers who stripped him and strung him up by the wrists to be flogged. He talked his way out of that ordeal, but then he was dragged before the city council to defend himself. His plans and prospects wilted under the threat of prolonged imprisonment, crippling legal threats, and likely execution.

Put yourself in his place—a disrupted life bound up in legal challenges, probable imprisonment, and waves of financial and physical strain.

But at that perilous moment Paul had a jailhouse visitor whose presence changed everything. Acts 23:11 says, "The following night the Lord stood near Paul and said, 'Take courage! As you have testified about me in Jerusalem, so you must also testify in Rome.'"

Notice those words, "The Lord *stood near* Paul and said . . ." Those words imply some sort of physical reality, an actual presence there behind prison walls, standing beside Paul as truly as a human personage. The word *Lord* is typically the way the New Testament writers designated Jesus Christ. This near-at-hand Lord spoke with commanding reassurance, saying: "Take courage! As you have testified about me in Jerusalem, so you must also testify in Rome."

When you turn to Jesus, He comes, stands beside you, is present by His Spirit, speaks through His Word, wards off fear, imparts courage, and reassures you about His promises and plans. That's what Paul experienced in Acts 23:11; in Philippians 4:5–6 he passed the lesson on to us: "The Lord is ever present with us. Don't be anxious about things; instead, pray" (THE VOICE).

It's true that God is everywhere at once, omnipresent, in every location of every realm in the visible and invisible spheres. God is not measurable, and the essence of His personality fills the galaxies and extends beyond the limits of the universe, traversing all the territories of fathomless infinity. He occupies every address, inhabits every sector, tracks every vector, and resides in every corner of the universe. He fills heaven and earth.

Yet in a personal way, our Lord draws near and speaks to us in times of stress, worry, anxiety, or fear. As I look back over my adult life, I've often been overtaken by anxiety. I've had times when I almost suffocated with worry. But what I remember most about those times is how they drove me to sit down, open my Bible, cry out to the Lord, pray to Him, and find specific Bible verses that calmed me down and gave me strength and courage. Those have become my favorite verses today.

That's the privilege of every Christian, and it's not just a matter of studying a book. It's a matter of meeting with a living Person and touching an unseen hand. Even now, I'm writing these words in an empty hotel room in Sioux City, Iowa, and I've been fighting off some nagging worries. But this isn't an empty hotel room. It's as full of the Lord's presence as the Holy of Holies. When I remind myself of that, reality enters the picture.

When I forget God's presence, I'm living in a state of denial, pretense, and error. When I practice His presence, I'm dealing with reality, and reality fosters peace.

I once read in a newspaper what happened to Blossie Anderson, a spunky eighty-five-year-old great-grandmother who decided to go fishing along the Saluda River near Greenville, South Carolina. When her sixty-two-year-old son, Louis, tried to dissuade her, she said, "I had you; you didn't have me."

Trudging into the snake-infested swamp with her fishing pole, she fell, struggled back to her feet, became disoriented, and waded through the area in the wrong direction. She finally sat down exhausted, hoping someone would come for her. "I wasn't afraid," she said, "I knew the Lord was with me, and I knew the Lord would bring help, so I just waited."

She waited all day long, and then she spent the night in the wild. The sun rose, and another day came and went. Meanwhile, rescuers mounted an extensive search, but they were looking on the wrong side of the river. The elderly woman just sat where she was, waiting and reminding herself that God was near her.

Rescue workers dragged the river for her body and kept searching. Four days later a rescuer thrashing around the area heard an elderly voice calling, "Hey, mister." The rescuer said, "Granny! How are you?"

"Lord have mercy," she replied, "I've been here for four days without anything to eat." She was taken to Greenville General Hospital where she was treated for exhaustion and dehydration and released. She later told reporters, "I slept at night and rested during the day. I wasn't cold, and I wasn't afraid of them snakes. God was with me, keeping me warm and keeping the snakes' jaws shut."[1]

God's very real presence sustained her. Now, don't ask me why He waited four days before having her rescued. The important thing is, He was with her. And don't ask me why you and I are sometimes swamped, stranded, and surrounded by snakes of one sort or another, for longer than we want. Every believer from biblical times until today has experienced disorienting days—but never a day when the Lord wasn't with us, keeping us warm and keeping the snakes' jaws shut.

Several categories of verses teach us this truth.

The *Nearness* Verses

- Psalm 73:28 says, "As for me, it is good to be *near* God."
- Psalm 145:18 says, "The LORD is *near* to all who call on him, to all who call on him in truth."
- Moses told the Israelites in Deuteronomy 4:7, "What other nation is so great as to have their gods *near*

them the way the LORD our God is *near* us whenever we pray to him?"

- The psalmist, when beset by foes, said, "Yet you are *near*, LORD, and all your commands are true" (Psalm 119:151).
- Jeremiah said, "You came *near* when I called you, and you said, 'Do not fear'" (Lamentations 3:57).
- Ephesians 2:13 says, "Now in Christ Jesus you who once were far away have been brought *near* by the blood of Christ."
- Hebrews 10:22 says, "Let us draw *near* to God with a sincere heart and with the full assurance that faith brings, having our hearts sprinkled to cleanse us from a guilty conscience."
- James added, "Draw near to God and He will draw *near* to you" (James 4:8 NKJV).
- And this is the word Paul chose to use in Philippians 4:5: "The Lord is *near*."

The *Presence* Verses

- Exodus 33:14 says, "My *presence* will go with you, and I will give you rest."
- Psalm 46:1 says, "God is our refuge and strength, an ever-*present* help in trouble."
- Psalm 140:13: "Surely the righteous will praise your name, and the upright will live in your *presence*."
- Psalm 16:11 says, "You make known to me the path

of life; you will fill me with joy in your *presence*, with eternal pleasures at your right hand."

- Psalm 89:15 speaks of the blessings enjoyed by those who walk in the light of God's *presence*.

- Acts 3:19 promises times of refreshment in the *presence* of the Lord. And when Paul exhorted Timothy in his ministry, he did it "in the *presence* of God and of Christ Jesus" (2 Timothy 4:1).

The *With* Verses

- When the patriarch Joseph was imprisoned in Egypt, the recurring theme was: "the LORD was *with* him" (Genesis 39:2, 3, 21, 23).

- Isaiah 41:10 says, "Do not fear, for I am *with* you."

- Genesis 28:15 says, "I am *with* you and will watch over you wherever you go."

- Isaiah 57:15 says, "This is what the high and exalted One says—he who lives forever, whose name is holy: 'I live in a high and holy place, but also *with* the one who is contrite and lowly in spirit.'"

- Psalm 23:4 says, "Even though I walk through the darkest valley, I will fear no evil, for you are *with* me."

- In a similar fashion, Deuteronomy 31:6 says, "Be strong and courageous. Do not be afraid or terrified because of them, for the LORD your God goes *with* you; he will never leave you nor forsake you."

- The gospel of Matthew begins by giving us a special

name for our Lord Jesus—Immanuel, which means "God *with* us" (1:23)—and Matthew ended his gospel with these final words of Jesus: "And surely I am *with* you always, to the very end of the age" (28:20).

The *Close* Verses

- Psalm 34:18 says, "The LORD is *close* to the brokenhearted and saves those who are crushed in spirit."
- Proverbs 18:24 says, "There is a friend who sticks *closer* than a brother."
- Isaiah 40:11 says, "He tends his flock like a shepherd: He gathers the lambs in his arms and carries them *close* to his heart."

The psalmist put this in personal terms when he prayed:

> Where can I go from your Spirit?
> > Where can I flee from your presence?
> If I go up to the heavens, you are there;
> > if I make my bed in the depths, you are
> > > there.
> If I rise on the wings of the dawn,
> > if I settle on the far side of the sea,
> even there your hand will guide me,
> > your right hand will hold me fast. (Psalm
> > > 139:7–10)

Hebrews 13:5–6 says, "'Never will I leave you; never will I forsake you.' So we say with confidence, 'The Lord is my helper; I will not be afraid.'"

In a sense, learning to actualize God's presence is the very definition of revival. Perhaps like you, I'm longing for a new great tsunami of revival to flood our land. (After everything we've been through in the past couple of years, I'm thinking, *The sooner the better!*) In my studies of the great revivals of the past, the most significant aspect is an intense, unusual, almost supernatural awareness of God's proximity.

Mrs. Hester Rendall told me of working with Rev. Duncan Campbell in the 1950s on the Hebrides island of Lewis. There had been an intense revival there between 1949 and 1952. Though Hester didn't arrive until 1958, the afterglow of the revival was still evident. One evening she went to a church service and a sense of the presence of the Lord came down so strongly that the people prayed earnestly and hardly dared lift their heads. After a while, Hester's friend leaned over to her and suggested they go home. Hester said, "Why? We've only been here a few minutes."

The friend said, "It's three o'clock in the morning."

Those who study revivals come across story after story like that, in which the intensity of the presence of God comes into a geographical zone so strongly that people are awed by it and are brought to instant conviction, conversion, and confidence. More than a hundred years ago, Frank Bartleman described a revival meeting he attended like this: "God came so wonderfully near us the very atmosphere of heaven seemed to surround us. Such a divine 'weight of glory' was upon us, we could only lie on our faces. . . . The Lord seemed almost visible, He was so real."

During the days of evangelist Charles Finney, a revival broke out in Rome, New York, and, according to historian Wesley Duewel, everyone who came into the village felt an overwhelming sense of God's presence. The sheriff of Utica, some twenty miles away, came on business. He had laughed and mocked at the reports of the revival. As his sleigh crossed the canal one mile outside Rome, an awesome feeling of the presence of God gripped him. The nearer to the village he came, the more powerfully he sensed God's presence. The sheriff found the people in the business establishments so overcome with awe for God they could hardly speak. To try to keep from weeping, the sheriff got up several times and went to the window. He hurried to complete his business and hastened back to Utica. Soon he was converted.

In some revivals, people have sensed the presence of God so powerfully that they "felt as if the Lord had breathed upon them." And according to one eyewitness during the 1906 Welsh revival, "a sense of the Lord's presence was everywhere. It pervaded, nay, it created the spiritual atmosphere. It mattered not where one went, the consciousness of the reality and nearness of God followed . . . in the homes, on the streets, in the mines and factories, in the schools."[2]

I've never had an experience quite as dramatic as those, but I am learning to recognize God's abiding presence by faith. As wonderful as these revival accounts are, they were momentary reminders of an enduring truth—the Lord is within us, around us, shielding, hovering over, accompanying, abiding with, and attending to us at all times, whether we can physically sense His presence or not. We walk by faith, not by feelings, but that doesn't diminish the reality of His nearness. He has so often reassured us of His presence, how could we doubt Him?

It helps to visualize His nearness. When you awaken in the morning, He is there. When you shower and dress to stagger on to work or school, He is there. When you board the plane, He is there. When the phone rings, He is there. When you get a bad report, He is there. When you face a difficult person, He is there. As you press through the day, working or resting, He is there. As you turn the doorknob and reenter your house at night, He is there. As you retire and go to bed, He is there.

Dr. A. W. Tozer explained, "The practice of the presence of God consists not of projecting an imaginary object from within [our] own mind and then seeking to realize its presence; it is rather to recognize the real presence of the One whom all sound theology declares to be already there."[3]

The chief purpose of prayer is to recognize the presence of the Lord. Someone once asked evangelist Dwight L. Moody how he managed to remain so intimate in his relationship with Christ. He replied,

> I have come to Him as the best friend I have ever found, and I can trust Him in that relationship. I have believed He is Savior; I have believed He is God; I have believed His atonement on the cross is mine, and I have come to Him and submitted myself on my knees, surrendered everything to Him, and got up and stood by His side as my friend, and there isn't any problem in my life, there isn't any uncertainty in my work but I turn and speak to Him as naturally as to someone in the same room, and I have done it these years because I can trust Jesus.[4]

THE LORD'S COMING IS NEAR

In the New Testament, the word *near* was sometimes used in connection with the return of Jesus Christ to earth, and several commentaries suggest this was on Paul's mind as he wrote Philippians 4:5.

In Matthew 24, for example, Jesus listed the "signs of the times" that would herald the nearness of His return, then He said, "Even so, when you see all these things, you know that it [My coming] is near, right at the door" (v. 33).

James added, "You too, be patient and stand firm, because the Lord's coming is near" (James 5:8).

Peter said, "The end of all things is near. Therefore be alert and of sober mind so that you may pray" (1 Peter 4:7).

The book of Revelation begins and ends by declaring our Lord's coming is near at hand (Revelation 1:3; 22:10).

You may say, "Those words were written nearly two thousand years ago, and Jesus still hasn't come. That doesn't seem like 'near' to me. If believers in New Testament days thought Jesus would return any moment, but He didn't come as they expected, why should we still be looking for Him now?"

Great question.

First, the Bible was written from God's perspective, and His concept of *nearness* is different from ours. To God, the time between our Lord's first and second comings is just a moment. From the vantage point of eternity, it's just a day or two. Peter pointed this out to critics in the first century who were impatient for the Lord's return and who demanded, "Where is this 'coming' he promised?" (2 Peter 3:4).

Peter replied, "Do not forget this one thing, dear friends: With the Lord a day is like a thousand years, and a thousand years are like a day. The Lord is not slow in keeping his promise, as some understand slowness" (vv. 8–9).

To our everlasting God, a thousand years resemble the passing of a single day. From the vantage of eternity, then,

Jesus has only been gone from earth a couple of days. He understands nearness and slowness from a different frame of reference. We dwell in time, but we share Christ's everlasting life. Believers in every generation have expected Jesus to come in their lifetimes, which is how it should be. The Lord wants us to live with anticipation and readiness, and, from His perspective, we may well be down to the last hours or minutes. His coming is soon, as He understands soon-ness, and that's good enough for me.

Second, there is a potentially more immediate nearness to our reunion with the Savior. If He doesn't come to us during our lifetimes, we will go to be with Him at the end of our lifetimes, and that could happen at any second. None of us has the promise of tomorrow. Every human on our planet is subject to sudden death at any moment, and Christians are not excluded. The possibility of our being reunited with our Lord is imminent, either through His sudden coming to us or through our departure to be with Him.

Sometimes when I'm overwhelmed with worry or with the weight of my problems, I remind myself that fifty years from now, I'll not be worried about any of this. When the Lord takes His children out of the world, they're released from all their problems, and this provides great solace. Jesus told the thief on the cross beside Him, "Truly I tell you, today you will be with me in paradise" (Luke 23:43).

One of the things we most look forward to about

heaven is freedom from every worry, anxiety, and care. Revelation 21:4 says, "'He will wipe every tear from their eyes. There will be no more death or mourning or crying or pain, for the old order of things has passed away.'"

We're presently part of the old order of things. We've living under a curse that fell across the universe because of sin. But for Christ followers, our problems are temporary and our burdens are momentary, but our blessings are permanent. Whatever we're worrying about now will someday be of no concern to us. God will release us from all our troubles and work them all for our good. He'll take over our problems and resolve them for His glory, and we can rest in a glorious future. The hymnist said:

> *Not now, but in the coming years,*
> *It may be in the better land,*
> *We'll read the meaning of our tears,*
> *And there, some time, we'll understand.*[5]

Two great verses of the Bible make this point:

- "I consider that our present sufferings are not worth comparing with the glory that will be revealed in us" (Romans 8:18).
- "For our light and momentary troubles are achieving for us an eternal glory that far outweighs them all" (2 Corinthians 4:17).

These are remarkable verses to ponder. Compared to the endless joys and untroubled life we're anticipating in heaven, our worst problems are, from that perspective, "light and momentary" and "not worth comparing with the glory that will be revealed."

This mindset infuses Philippians 4:5 with meaning, and, indeed, it illumines the whole atmosphere of Paul's letter to the Philippians. He began the book with his great personal statement of purpose:

> For to me, to live is Christ and to die is gain. If I am to go on living in the body, this will mean fruitful labor for me. Yet what shall I choose? I do not know! I am torn between the two: I desire to depart and be with Christ, which is better by far; but it is more necessary for you that I remain in the body. (1:21–24)

In other words, Paul relished the prospects of going to heaven, leaving behind all his stresses and strains and pains. He was eager to be rid of his worries and to be with the Lord, which would be better for him by far. Yet he felt God still had some remaining fruitful labor for him on this planet, so he was willing to stay earthbound awhile longer.

Later, in Philippians 3, in discussing his adversaries, Paul wrote:

> As I have often told you . . . , many live as enemies of the cross of Christ. Their destiny is destruction, their god is

> their stomach, and their glory is in their shame. Their
> mind is set on earthly things. But our citizenship is in
> heaven. And we eagerly await a Savior from there, the
> Lord Jesus Christ, who, by the power that enables him to
> bring everything under his control, will transform our
> lowly bodies so that they will be like his glorious body.
> (vv. 18–21)

When I was a little boy, ten or eleven years old, my
dad promised to take us to Myrtle Beach, South Carolina,
on vacation. We'd been there before, and I can't tell you
how excited I was. I loved going to Myrtle Beach, chowing
down on pancakes in the morning, playing in the ocean
all day, riding everything at the carnival in the evening,
playing miniature golf, and having my parents' full attention for the whole week.

My little sister, Ann, was about five, and I wanted
her to be as excited about the trip as I was. I wrote to the
Myrtle Beach Chamber of Commerce asking for brochures. A week or so later, I began getting brochures by
the dozens from every attraction, amusement park, hotel,
restaurant, and golf course on the Grand Strand. I organ-
ized them on a folding table and went over every brochure
with Ann. I had her so excited she could hardly sleep at
night. We were so wound up with anticipation, we almost
could have flown there by flapping our arms.

In the week before we left, I might have gotten into

trouble with my parents. One of those lost library books might have plagued me. Maybe I had a flat tire on my bicycle. I probably scraped my knee. But I recovered from all such problems more quickly because I was busy packing for the beach. The anticipation of the trip eclipsed everything else in my life.

I still love going to Myrtle Beach, and I get great joy anticipating other trips as well. But there's one destination I'm looking forward to above all. In times of anxiety or distress I remind myself, "None of these problems are going to matter to me in a few years. All my worries are short-lived, and in any event, God has promised they will somehow turn out for good."

Abraham lived in tents and weathered the troubles of life by faith, "for he was looking forward to the city with foundations, whose architect and building is God . . . longing for a better country—a heavenly one" (Hebrews 11:10, 16).

Can you see how eternal anticipation is an antidote to current frustration? The regular contemplation of the Lord's return and of heaven is an essential biblical therapy for anxiety. The Bible is all about the future. Page after page and passage after passage is devoted to prophecy, to what's ahead, to the resurrection, to the return of Christ, to the endless adventures of everlasting life.

The next time you fall into an anxious state, take a deep breath, put your problem on hold, find a quiet spot, and read Revelation 21–22, which is the Bible's travel brochure of heaven. Picture the diamond city of New Jerusalem descending like a jewel to the new earth. Visualize the streets, walls, gates, throne, and crystal river. Read 1 Thessalonians 4 about the moment of Christ's return. Study prophecy. See what the Bible says about the future. Our burdens cannot follow us to heaven, and our trials and troubles are not worth comparing to the glory that will be revealed in us.

Whatever your burdens today, remember to practice joy, dependence, and nearness, both in terms of Christ's imminent coming and His immediate presence. According to God Himself, those are great first responses anytime you are besieged by anxiety.

CHAPTER 4

The Habit of Gratitude

J ohn Brockman is a literary agent and scientific writer who specializes in bringing together the planet's best minds to contribute to his website and online magazine. He's renowned for his access to Nobel Prize winners, brilliant thinkers, and world-class scientists and technologists. Few, if any, of these thinkers are Christians, but they all make interesting contributions to Brockman's journal.

Every year on the anniversary of the launch of his website, Brockman and his editors craft a different question and invite their high-octane participants to answer it. The questions vary from year to year, but they're always remarkably perceptive. One year the question was very simple: "What should we be worried about?"

One professor said he's worried because "global cooperation is failing and we don't know why."[1] Another is anxious because we're "living in a world of cascading crises."[2]

Another contributor said he was concerned with the "Unknown Unknowns" ahead of us, and yet anther eminent professor had a one-word title for his essay: "Armageddon."[3]

Interestingly enough, this question was posed in 2013, and yet answers like these could just as easily have come from the 2020 archives.

Before Covid came along, few of us lost sleep over cosmic threats until they were brought home to us in an immediate way. Most of our worries were closer at hand. But the pandemic merged these two realms of "cosmic" and "close" into one. A global crisis showed up in our neighborhoods and homes, and ever since, we've lived painfully aware of inhabiting an anxious world that skips along the edges of danger and difficulty. We've seen it for ourselves firsthand— no one knows what the next hour or day will bring. Yet the Bible directs us to live beyond the fear and to make gratitude (which Scripture often refers to as "thanksgiving") a priority.

Former Miss America, Debbye Turner Bell, battled understandably difficult emotions when her mother died. "My body hurt. My mind ached. My thoughts spun out of control. I kept replaying that last doctor's visit, the last time I saw my mom, the last time I talked with her. I wondered what I should have done differently. Curiously, for a long time afterwards, I thought my mom's death was somehow my fault."

Debbye went to the Lord in prayer, and she told the Lord of her anger and frustration, but her pain was overwhelming.

One night, I couldn't sleep because of the horror of my mom's death. My prayers seemed to be hitting the ceiling and falling back down around me. Since they didn't seem to be getting through to God, I decided to read my Bible. I couldn't think of a Scripture, so I picked up the Bible and let it fall open randomly. I closed my eyes, pointed my index finger, and let it fall to a spot on the page.

I opened my eyes and my gaze fell on: "Be anxious for nothing, but in everything by prayer and supplication, with thanksgiving, let your requests be made known to God; and the peace of God, which surpasses all understanding, will guard your hearts and minds through Christ Jesus" (Philippians 4:6–7).

Debbye prayed earnestly for God's supernatural peace, and she fell asleep with her Bible on her chest. When she awakened the next morning, she felt a release, a joy, a peace that she couldn't understand or explain.[4]

That's why Debbye follows her mom's example of consistent thanksgiving. "I still start my days with prayer," she says. "No matter how early I rise or how busy the day, the moment I open my eyes, I thank God for another day and ask for wisdom to get me through whatever life may bring."[5]

THE THEOLOGY OF GRATITUDE

Sometimes our fears and worries feel more like wolves circling us in the dark than little creatures nibbling away at our peace. In a world where we've been anxious over everything from the fragility of complex systems to the availability of hospital beds and baby formula, we need to nurture thankful hearts and minds full of gratitude.

To approach any situation, any dilemma, any frightening report "with thanksgiving" adds a dimension that melts away anxiety like winter's ice on a sunny day. No matter our crisis or concern, there are always notable items for which we can be thankful, and finding them is critical to winning the fight. If we don't find those items and thank God for them, we cannot overcome anxiety. Gratitude is to worry what antibiotics are to an infection. The old practice of "counting our blessings" is an effective modern treatment for what ails the mind. Giving thanks is essential to mental health.

I believe that's what the apostle Paul learned as well. As we've already speculated, he seemed, by nature, highstrung and keyed up. But Paul had learned to weave the concept of "with thanksgiving" into the fabric of his thinking, and gratitude appeared incessantly in his writing.

He spoke of it in theological terms, as though it were as important as any other doctrine.

This shows up clearly in his letter to the Colossians where, throughout its four chapters, we find Paul's theology of gratitude—which, incidentally, had also become a *habit* of gratitude—on every page.

"We always *thank God*," the apostle wrote in Colossians 1:3. Then down in verse 10, Paul commanded the Colossians: "Live a life worthy of the Lord and please him in every way." We do that by:

> bearing fruit in every good work, growing in the knowledge of God, being strengthened with all power according to his glorious might so that you may have great endurance and patience, and *giving joyful thanks to the Father,* who has qualified you to share in the inheritance of his holy people in the kingdom of light. (vv. 10–12)

Colossians 2 continues the theme: "So then, just as you received Christ Jesus as Lord, continue to live your lives in him, rooted and built up in him, strengthened in the faith as you were taught, and *overflowing with thankfulness*" (vv. 6–7).

Imagine you were a river. If thanksgiving were measured like water, would you be a dry gulch, a trickle, brimming at the banks, or overflowing at flood stage? How you and I answer that simple question says something about our mental health and our ability to manage our anxieties.

The next chapter of Colossians extends the connection between gratitude and peace of mind: "Let the peace of Christ rule in your hearts. . . . And *be thankful*. . . . And whatever you do, whether in word or deed, do it all in the name of the Lord Jesus, *giving thanks* to God the Father through him" (3:15–17).

Then we come to Colossians 4, which commands, "Devote yourselves to prayer, being watchful and *thankful*" (v. 2).

This theme isn't just found in Colossians, of course. It runs like a stream from the first pages of Scripture to the last ones, and it's interlaced into the Bible as fully as any doctrine. Dr. Al Mohler wrote, "Thanksgiving is a deeply theological act, rightly understood. As a matter of fact, thankfulness is theology in microcosm—a key to understanding what we really believe about God, ourselves, and the world we experience."[6]

THE PSYCHOLOGY OF GRATITUDE

The great Bible teacher Harry Ironside said, "We would worry less if we praised more. Thanksgiving is the enemy of discontent and dissatisfaction."[7] In simplest terms, that means you can instantly lessen the level of your anxiety by finding something for which to immediately thank God. It works like this for me: If something triggers an anxious episode, I have to pull myself together and ask, "As bad as this seems, it's not as bad as it could be. In fact, here are some things I can thank God for in the middle of this mess." I then use my brainpower to compile a list of blessings.

It's like the seesaw we played on as children. When the poundage at one end counterbalances the other, the law of gravity goes into effect. The weight of our blessings is sometimes heavy enough to flip our worries into the air like a bully caught off guard.

This is classic Christianity, but something interesting has happened in recent times in the secular world. An entire science of gratitude has arisen, as legions of experts are discovering the psychological power of gratitude. Most of these modern scholars aren't coming at thanksgiving and gratitude from a distinctively Christian point of view, but they're nonetheless discovering how this biblical attitude, lived out daily, has a profound effect on the human spirit.

One of the foremost researchers in this field is Dr. Robert A. Emmons of the University of California, Davis. In his book *Thanks! How Practicing Gratitude Can Make You Happier*, he explained how everyone is born with certain preset elements to their personality. Just as each of us has a unique and individual body, so each of us has a unique and individual personality. Some are more introverted; some more extroverted. Some are strong-willed; others are acquiescent. Some are more inclined to be happy; some are prone toward melancholy. In fact, according to Dr. Emmons, "Current psychological dogma states that one's capacity for joy is biologically set."[8]

"Each person appears to have a set-point for happiness," he writes. "Each person has a chronic or characteristic level of happiness . . . to which they inevitably return following disruptive life events."[9]

But Dr. Emmons's innovative research has demonstrated that there is one quality that, if developed and practiced, can actually change our set-point for happiness. We can change the gauges of our personalities in an upward and happier direction if we deliberately and doggedly work on improving our habit of giving thanks.

Emmons wrote:

> We discovered scientific proof that when people regularly engage in a systematic cultivation of gratitude, they experience a variety of measurable benefits: psychological, physical, and interpersonal. The evidence on gratitude contradicts the widely held view that all people have a "set-point" of happiness that cannot be reset by any known means: in some cases, people have reported that gratitude led to transformative life changes.[10]

He concluded, "Our groundbreaking research has shown that grateful people experience higher levels of positive emotions such as joy, enthusiasm, love, happiness and optimism, and that the practice of gratitude as a discipline protects a person from the destructive impulses of envy, resentment, greed, and bitterness."[11]

Another book on this subject is *The Gratitude Diaries* by Janice Kaplan, who, while an editor-in-chief of *Parade* magazine, led a survey funded by the John Templeton Foundation on the subject of gratitude and its impact. Her research became personal to her, and she was affected by something she read in the *Journal of Social and Clinical Psychology*: "Gratitude may have the highest connection to mental health and happiness of any of the personality traits studied."[12]

Kaplan determined to become her own social scientist. "I wanted to see what happened when I developed an attitude of gratitude," she said. Instead of doing this casually, she determined to make a full commitment to get as much information as she could in addition to modifying her own behavior. She would then report and record her findings.

Kaplan sought advice at every turn from experts and psychologists, and she consulted books by philosophers and psychologists and theologians.[13] She also took up one of Dr. Emmons's suggested habits, noting that a consistent finding in the research was "the value of keeping a gratitude journal. Researchers have found," she said, "that people who write down three things they're grateful for every night (or even a few times a week) improve their well-being and lower their risk of depression. The results have been repeated over and over. Keeping a gratitude journal can even dramatically improve your ability to get a good night's sleep."[14]

Kaplan conducted her own one-year experiment, and the subtitle of her book summarizes her findings: *The Gratitude Diaries: How a Year Looking on the Bright Side Can Transform Your Life.*

THE METHODOLOGY OF GRATITUDE

As a pastor, I'm tempted to feel some fiendish delight when modern researchers spend large sums of money to "discover" something the Bible announced long ago. But as it relates to studying gratitude, secular researchers run into an impassable roadblock when they try to answer the question: "To whom are we thankful?" They may uncover the benefits of feeling thankful, but how can we be thankful to a purely impersonal universe?

We can always be thankful to certain people who love or befriend us. But what about all the blessings that can't be credited to friends, loved ones, or ruling authorities? What about the wonders of sky, sea, and land? What about life itself, the privilege of living on a spinning blue marble in a vast universe of fathomless complexity?

The ability to say, "Thank You, Lord," is among the most wonderful things about being a follower of Jesus Christ. We can enter His gates with thanksgiving and

His courts with praise. We don't thank and praise God merely to gain the psychological benefits of doing so. We thank and praise Him because He is the God from whom all blessings flow. But this gratitude boomerangs into benefits the world can never know. Emotional benefits. Psychological blessings. And spiritual experiences such as the peace and hope of Christ.

What a tragedy if, as Jesus followers, we fail to truly thank God in a Christlike way for all His blessings. The Lutheran minister Martin Rinkart wrote a hymn of thanksgiving to rally his village of Ellenburg, Saxony, during the ravages of the Thirty Years' War. Rinkart was the only surviving pastor in town, and he sometimes conducted as many as fifty funerals a day. Yet he kept himself and his village sane by finding items of thanksgiving, even among the carnage. He converted this attitude into one of our great hymns:

> *Now thank we all our God, with*
> *heart and hands and voices,*
> *Who wondrous things has done, in*
> *whom his world rejoices;*
> *Who from our mothers' arms has blessed us on our way*
> *With countless gifts of love, and still is ours today.*[15]

How can we cultivate a spirit of gratitude like that? My friend Linda Derby once faced a health crisis in her family. Her daughter-in-law, Becky, mother of two little boys, was diagnosed with cancer, and it was a devastating case. On the day they received the bad news, Linda said it felt as if a black cloud of poisonous insects was swarming around her head, and she was panicked with fear.

She later wrote:

As I sought God and started to pray, He brought to mind the words of the Apostle Paul to the Philippians: "Don't worry about anything; instead, pray about everything. Tell God what you need, and thank him for all he has done. Then you will experience God's peace, which exceeds anything we can understand" (Philippians 4:6–7 NLT).

After this epiphany, I decided to really get serious about talking to God. I started telling Him everything our family was experiencing, our worries, anxiety, fear, depression, anger, and uncertainty—I told God what we wanted, such as peace and assurance that Becky would be all right. Then I tried to think of all the things God had done that I was thankful for. . . . To my surprise, there were many good things that had recently happened.[16]

She went on to list five distinct blessings, and she was surprised at how she had nearly overlooked them. By the end of the evening, she said, the cloud of insects had been swept away by the Spirit of God and she was able to go to bed with peace in her heart and enjoy a restful night of sleep.[17]

If Linda had omitted that last step of thanksgiving, a few of those insects would have buzzed through her mind all night. "With thanksgiving" is an indelible aspect of Scripture and an invaluable habit for dispelling the cloud of anxiety from our minds.

Here are some ideas I've gleaned from others and tried for myself in my efforts to develop a stronger habit of gratitude.

- **Keep a thanksgiving list.** I've been doing this for many years, ever since I read about the British hymnist Frances Ridley Havergal, who kept one alongside her prayer list. Every morning I begin my prayer time by writing down something for which I'm grateful to the Lord.
- **Before you fall asleep at night, thank God for three things that happened during the day.** I don't remember where I learned this little technique, but I've been practicing it regularly. In this way, I begin the day with one item of thanksgiving and end it with three. It puts my mind in a better place before I fall asleep.
- **Keep a gratitude journal.** This is the chief tool used by psychologists like Dr. Emmons. They suggest keeping a small notebook in which you

write down one, two, or three things each day for which you're thankful.

- **Give thanks at meals.** We have three natural opportunities a day to express our gratitude to the Lord. You can be specific. "Lord, thank You for this bowl of beans and cornbread." Remember that every good and perfect gift comes down from above, from the Father of lights, from whom there is no shadow or variation (James 1:17).

- **Whenever you encounter a disappointment or disaster, try to specifically locate and list items for which you can be thankful, even in the midst of the problem.** The Bible says, "Give thanks in all circumstances; for this is God's will for you in Christ Jesus" (1 Thessalonians 5:18). "*In* all circumstances" doesn't mean "*for* all circumstances." This is sometimes where people get unnecessarily frustrated or discouraged. One way to understand this verse is as a call to give thanks *during* all circumstances. Whatever items you think of to be grateful for during those times, write them in your journal, in your calendar, or in a text to yourself—whatever works to focus your mind on them.

- **Express your gratitude to others.** Let people at

work know that you're grateful for their work. Studies have shown that offices are the least common places to hear or express gratitude, and when we express our appreciation to coworkers it increases the overall effectiveness of the organization.[18] The same is true, of course, at home, church, or school.

- **Read books on gratitude.** I've mentioned a couple of them in this chapter. Whenever I study a subject, the topic expands in my mind and heart.

- **Sing songs and hymns that inspire thanks.** Ephesians 5 tells us to be filled with the Spirit, speaking to one another with psalms, hymns, and spiritual songs, singing and making melody in our hearts to the Lord, giving thanks always for all things to God the Father in the name of our Lord Jesus Christ (vv. 18–21). If you're in a difficult place right now, find a song and sing it aloud. It might seem a little awkward, but keep doing it. Keep singing along. It will begin lifting your spirits.

- **Create a playlist.** It's no secret that "Now Thank We All Our God" is one of my personal favorites, but an online search of "thanksgiving hymns and songs" will bring up countless options across eras and music genres. And if you'll create your own playlist, you'll have these songs handy anytime you're needing them.

- **Memorize some thanksgiving passages.** Psalm 100 is a good place to begin. That's the psalm that says, "Enter his gates with thanksgiving and his courts with praise; give thanks to him and praise his name. For the LORD is good and his love endures forever; his faithfulness continues through all generations."

Dr. J. Sidlow Baxter recalled a time when, at age eighty-eight, he was asked to speak at a large church in Memphis. He told the group he had been struggling with difficult issues related to his age and health and nerves. He spoke of being on a preaching tour of Scotland when he slumped into a period of deep despondency. "Everything seemed upsetting and frustrating and foreboding."[19] He was also overwhelmed with his workload and shaken by several recent disappointments.

One night, he said,

I went to bed weary with mental wrestling and frustration. And then, somewhere between night and morning, September 6th and 7th, something happened that changed everything. I heard no audible voice, but someone had wakened me amid the curtains of the night; and was speaking within me. By a language which I knew at once. He said, "Sid! Sid! . . . You've been forgetting the thanksgiving. Hand everything over to Me, Sid. And start praying again with thanksgiving."[20]

Baxter said,

I can't explain it too coherently but that is just what I did. In bed, there and then, amid the nocturnal darkness I handed everything over to Him. And I started praying again with thanksgiving. . . . And I saw everything with illuminating difference and clearness. My mental tension and gloom had gone.[21]

The next morning Baxter found that his entire nervous system had become relaxed. He said, "As I prayed with thanksgiving—I could never forget it—the peace of God invaded my heart like a gentle zephyr."[22]

You and I need the same experience, and it's available from the God of all peace. The same God who has calmed the anxiety of His loved ones since the beginning of time. How about entering His gates with thanksgiving today, and letting gratitude have its glorious effect in you?

CHAPTER 5

The Habit of Thinking

I was on a flight to Toronto beside a woman whose nose was in a book. I hunkered down in the window seat with my Bible and notepad and studied through the flight. We didn't chat until time to land, at which point she looked over and commented about my studying the Bible. I told her I enjoyed studying the Bible very much. She told me she was the national director of human resources for a large automotive company, and that she had read her Bible in younger years. On one occasion, she said, she had been asked to give a recitation. She had several choices of material, but she had chosen a passage from the Bible, and it had meant a great deal to her at the time.

"Oh," I said, "what passage did you read?"

"It was from, now, let me see . . . what was it? Fallopians?"

"You mean Philippians?"

"Yes," she said, "Philippians. Maybe it was . . . is there a chapter 4?"

"Was it this passage?" I asked, and then I quoted Philippians 4:4–9 to her, word for word, starting with its proclamation: "Rejoice in the Lord always. I will say it again: Rejoice!" To my surprise, the woman grew visibly emotional. She broke into tears and started fanning herself with her hands, saying, "I don't know what's happening to me. I'm not usually like this at all."

She hauled up her purse—it was the size of a small Saint Bernard—and began searching for a tissue, which was nowhere to be found. The tears ran down her cheeks and she mopped them up with her palms. I offered my handkerchief.

"I've been so busy and so stressed," she explained, wiping her eyes, "that I've been short with people recently and I've been demanding and difficult and worried. And here you are, quoting something to me I learned long ago and had forgotten. I guess I needed to remember those words again."

By the time she composed herself, we were being herded off the plane, all of us late for connecting flights. I didn't even get the woman's name. But what a blessing to share Scripture with her and to see the effect these simple words had on her thoughts and feelings. She badly needed to refocus her mind on truths she had learned long ago, but that had vanished from her memory like a dissipating mist.

When our minds are overtaken with worry, distress, or discouragement, there's only one thing to do. We have to remember. We have to call to mind the truths we need. We have to take control of our thoughts and stop listening to ourselves and start preaching to ourselves, lecturing ourselves, exhorting ourselves. In short, we learn to think on the things that the Lord says will uplift and minister to us.

That's what's recommended in one of the verses the woman on the plane had once memorized, Philippians 4:8: "Whatever is true, whatever is noble, whatever is right, whatever is pure, whatever is lovely, whatever is admirable—if anything is excellent or praiseworthy—think about such things." Out of all the words in that sentence, only one is an action verb, and it's the sole imperative—*think*.

Notice how important this is for the entirety of our life, not just for our anxiety. As Proverbs 23:7 puts it, "For as he thinketh in his heart, so is he" (KJV). Proverbs 4:23 warns, "Be careful how you think; your life is shaped by your thoughts (GNT). And in Isaiah 26:3, we read, "You will keep him in perfect peace, whose mind is stayed on You, because he trusts in You (NKJV).

This is an inescapable biblical fact. For better or for worse, our thoughts will mold our personalities and either move us further into the realm of God's peace or away from it.

Even non-Christians know this. If we have anxious thoughts, we'll be anxious people because what we *think* is the most important thing about us. Our lives, attitudes, feelings, reactions, results, failures, successes, and personalities are formed by the strands of thought that tie our brain cells together like baling wire. This is so self-evident, it's been at the heart of philosophy and religion from the beginning of human civilization.

- The Hindus teach, "Man becomes that of which he thinks."
- The Buddha said, "The mind is everything: what you think you become."
- Marcus Aurelius said, "Your life is what your thoughts make it."
- Descartes wrote: "I think, therefore I am."
- William James laid the foundation for today's motivational, positive-thinking movement with these simple words: "The greatest discovery of my generation is that human beings can alter their lives by altering their attitudes of mind."[1]
- The homespun British philosopher James Allen summed it up well, writing:

A man is literally what he thinks, his character being the complete sum of all his thoughts. . . . Good thoughts bear good fruit, bad thoughts bad fruit. . . . Let a man radically alter his thoughts, and he will be astonished at the rapid transformation it will effect in the material conditions of his life. Men imagine that thought can be kept secret, but it cannot; it rapidly crystallizes into habit, and habit solidifies into circumstances.[2] Allen added, "As the physically weak man can make himself strong by careful and patient training, so the man of weak thoughts can make them strong by exercising himself in right thinking."[3]

To calm our anxiety and win the war over worry, we must think rightly, on the right things, at the right time, with our antenna tuned to the frequency of God's truth. We cannot overcome anxiety unless we learn to replace *worried* thoughts with *worthy* thoughts—thoughts that come directly from the mind of the God of peace.

A RARE ACTIVITY

Thinking is an activity that's fallen on hard times. We're too busy to think, and our minds are congested with noise. It's hard to meditate with incoming messages arriving like missiles on our phones and watches and computers, and speakers and TVs blaring like the Tower of Babel.

We don't ride horses into town now. Our work isn't undertaken in quiet fields, disturbed by nothing beyond the murmur of the wind or the distant baying of a dog. We no longer read by the flicker of candlelight or the glow of a fire-place. That was lost long ago in the Industrial Revolution; now the Information and Technology Revolutions instantly deliver the cacophony of the world straight into our ear-drums via a billion earbuds and headphones. We rush through traffic like salmon bolting upstream to spawn. We're bombarded by noise and besieged by stimuli. Surround sound is a way of life, and lost to us—without true spiritual effort—is the spirit of Isaiah 30:15: "In quietness and confidence shall be your strength" (NKJV). Or Psalm 46:10: "Be still, and know that I am God."

If you'll listen quietly in His presence, the Lord
is whispering the same words to you.

Thinking is the Bible's great corrective for mind-lessness. One day during my freshman year in college, a visiting guru with a flowing robe and white beard arrived on campus touting the practice of transcendental medita-tion. His basic gist, as I recall, was to find moments when we could unwind our muscles, close our eyes, empty our minds, breathe deeply, and relax. I like relaxation and deep breathing, and those are important tools in combat-ing tension and anxiety. When we empty and refill our lungs, we're infusing our bloodstream with God's fresh air, which replenishes our brains, calms our moods, and fortifies our nerves.

But the guru was wrong about emptying one's mind.

By definition, *meditation* means "directing the mind to dwell on a certain thought," and Scripture is clear about the types of thoughts that can certainly help us. Our minds don't make good vacuum chambers. They need nourishing truth. So we want to develop minds that migrate, in their most natural and relaxed moments, to thoughts that are:

- True

    Truth is an attribute of God. Everything about Him is absolutely and utterly true, for He is truth. His truth is reflected in everything He has made throughout His universe. All of creation evidences measurable scientific facts, consistent laws, and immutable principles. Everything God says is utterly true, and every word in the Bible is absolutely and objectively true and trustworthy. These, then, are the things we should think about.

- Noble

    This is a royal word that conveys the nobility of a king. Sometimes this is translated "honorable," conveying the idea of dignity, good character, and worthy of respect. We should train our minds to dwell and daydream on whatever is noble.

- Right

    The meaning behind this word isn't simply "correct." It conveys the idea of being morally right, all right, upright. Think of it this way: our minds will be either *upright* or *uptight*, but it's hard for them to remain in both conditions for long.

- Pure

  In an age of epidemic pornography and immorality, God wants our minds to dwell on things that are pure. In the days of Noah, "The LORD saw how great the wickedness of the human race had become on the earth, and that every inclination of the thoughts of the human heart was only evil all the time" (Genesis 6:5). Only the power of God's true, noble, and right Word can reverse this. A steady habit of meditation on His Word day and night is the divine filtration system of the heart that keeps our thoughts pure.

- Lovely

  The first four letters of this word spell "love." It refers to things that are beautiful, eloquent, elegant, captivating, and appealing to our highest impulses.

- Admirable

  If you can't admire it, don't desire it.

- Excellent

  These are God's most outstanding truths. The apostle Paul used this word in Titus 3:8, when he told Titus to teach the true doctrines of Scripture.

"I want you to stress these things, so that those who have trusted God may be careful to devote themselves to doing what is good. These things are excellent and profitable for everyone."

- Praiseworthy

We should think about the God we praise—and about all the things we can praise Him for. "The highest science, the loftiest speculation, the mightiest philosophy which can ever engage the attention of a child of God is the name, the nature, the person, the work, the doings, and the existence of the great God whom he calls his Father," said Charles Haddon Spurgeon, adding that "there is something exceedingly improving to the mind in a contemplation of the Divinity. It is a subject so vast, that all our thoughts are lost in its immensity; so deep, that our pride is drowned in its infinity."[4]

HOW DO WE THINK ABOUT THESE THINGS?

In a sense, these eight words are a description of God Himself, and of Jesus Christ, who is the epitome of all that is true, noble, right, pure, lovely, admirable, excellent, and praiseworthy. According to 2 Corinthians 3:18, we are transformed by contemplating all He is and all He is for us: "And we all, who with unveiled faces contemplate the Lord's glory, are being transformed into his image with ever-increasing glory, which comes from the Lord, who is the Spirit."

These eight words also describe the scope of Scripture, which brings us back to the habits of Bible study, Scripture memorization , and contemplative meditation. Romans 8 says, "Those who live according to the flesh have their minds set on what the flesh desires; but those who live in accordance with the Spirit have their minds set on what the Spirit desires. The mind governed by the flesh is death, but the mind governed by the Spirit is life and peace" (vv. 5–6). Notice the word *peace*. When our minds are governed by the Spirit and filled with the Scripture, we're training them to move from panic to peace, from worry to worship, and from anxiety to confident trust.

That's why I'm a strong advocate for Scripture memory and meditation. I've written two books on these subjects—*100 Bible Verses Everyone Should Know by Heart* and *Reclaiming the Lost Art of Biblical Meditation.* The patterns I describe in these two books have transformed my life more than anything else I've ever discovered. They've helped me overcome temptation—especially the temptations of distress and discouragement—more than I can describe.

My own habits along these lines are very simple. As I suggested earlier, most mornings during my devotional time I spend a few minutes working on a phrase of a Bible memory verse. It's true we have instantaneous access to Scripture on our phones or tablets, and we can search for a verse with a few taps of a finger. But when we memorize a verse, it gets out of our phones or off the page of our books, and it's planted in the furrows of our conscious minds, where it sinks into our subconsciousness—and even into our unconscious thoughts.

When I decide on a verse to memorize, I write it in a little leather notebook and read it aloud over and over. Taking my phone, I punch the voice recorder and try quoting the first phrases, then I listen to see what I've missed. I do the same thing the next day. It may take me days, weeks, or even months to learn a passage, but all along the way the passage becomes more familiar. It becomes more deeply etched on the walls of my memory. I often go to sleep thinking about that verse, and I wake up thinking about it, and I think about it in the shower, and I think about it when driving or walking.

If I get a negative report, hear bad news, or have a panicked moment, I say, "Lord, You know I'm tensing up right now, but I'm claiming this verse"—and then quote it out loud.

You might want to post that verse or passage on the screen of your phone or with a sticky note to your makeup mirror or coffeepot. But what helps me is to learn it a phrase at a time. Think about those first few words as you prepare for the day. Turn them into a prayer or a simple song as you dress or put the cereal bowl in the dishwasher. Say them several times, emphasizing each word in turn.

As you drive home, repeat that phrase or sentence several times. Turn it into a prayer for others if possible. Draw a hot bath, sink into the water, and think of the words again. As you go to sleep, let that thought be the last conscious thing on your mind. Then, when you're ready, you can add the next phrase, and then the next.

Repeat the process verse by verse, and within a few weeks or months you'll have the entire passage stored away in your mind, written like calligraphy on your soul, always available, and constantly radiating its truths into the most private places of your heart.

One of the beautiful things about God's Word is that you cannot overuse it or wear it out. I've been thinking about certain scriptures I've shared in this book for decades, and I love them more now than when I first learned them.

Someone sent me a quote that says, "Look around and be distressed. Look within and be depressed. Look above and be at rest." One of the easiest ways of looking above is exploring the heavenly words between the covers of your Bible.

TRANSFORMATIONAL MEDITATION

Not until I transferred to Columbia International University as a sophomore did someone teach me Romans 12:2, a verse about being transformed by the renewing of our minds. I learned that what God desires for us isn't *transcendental* meditation, but *transformational* meditation.

As we internalize, visualize, and personalize God's Word, we're transformed into the kind of people He wants us to be. We see things from His perspective. We think increasingly as Jesus does, and our minds are deepened, sharpened, composed, and calmed. J. B. Phillips rendered Romans 12:2 like this: "Don't let the world around you squeeze you into its own mould, but let God re-mould your minds from within" (PHILLIPS).[5]

This strategy saved the life of missionary Geoffrey Bull, a Scottish expatriate who was captured and imprisoned by Chinese communists in Tibet. His possessions, including his Bible, were stripped from him and he was thrown into a series of prisons, where he suffered terribly for three years. In addition to extreme temperatures, scant food, and miserable conditions, Bull was subjected to such mental and psychological torture he feared he would go insane. But he had studied the Bible all his life, so he began to systematically go through Scripture in his mind.

He found it took him about six months to go all the way through the Bible mentally. He started at Genesis, and recalled each incident and story as best he could, first concentrating on the content and then musing on certain points, seeking light in prayer. He continued through the

Old Testament, reconstructing the books and chapters as best he could and focusing his thoughts on verses he knew by heart, then into the New Testament and on to Revelation. Then he started over again. He later wrote: "The strength received through this meditation was, I believe, a vital factor in bringing me through, kept by the faith to the very end."[6]

The great thing about internalizing Scripture through memorization and meditation is its power to transform us and even to convert our circumstances and surroundings from anxiety-inducing to praise-producing.

Why not start now with a passage from God's Word that is personally meaningful to you? As the months, years, and decades go by, you'll be weaving your favorite Bible verses into a blanket that will warm your heart and mind as long as you live and will furnish you endless encouragement to pass along to others. The Word of God will become ingrained into your personality like veins of gold.

EIGHT STEPS TO WRITING SCRIPTURE ON YOUR HEART AND MIND

When I teach this process of internalizing Scripture—writing it on one's heart and mind—to a group, I often break it down into eight simple steps.

1. **Passage.** Begin with a passage of Scripture

and read it over and over. One evening I was overcome with stress and fatigue and a sense of confusion, and I turned to Psalm 121, which I had memorized in the King James Version: "I will lift up mine eyes unto the hills, from whence cometh my help. My help cometh from the LORD, which made heaven and earth." I quoted that psalm to myself, looked it up, read it again, and adopted it as my passage for the evening.

2. **Probe.** Having found a passage to settle into, start reading it and studying it. I often type the passage out, print it, and dissect it using pens and pencils. In the case of Psalm 121, I noticed how the eight verses divide into four natural stanzas of two verses each, and I drew lines between them, noting how the logic of the psalm progresses from stanza to stanza.

3. **Ponder.** Then ponder the passage. First, what does this passage mean? Then consider: What does it mean to me? How would I explain it to someone else if I had the opportunity? How would I teach it, were I asked to lead a Bible study?

4. **Paint.** It's often helpful to paint a mental picture of the passage and use our imaginations to bring Scripture to life. For someone like me who grew up in the Appalachians, it's easy to think about lifting

our eyes up to the mountains. I can close my eyes and see the towering peaks, molded and formed by an infinite hand. The same God who made the ancient hills is nearby to establish my peace, settle my soul, and grant His help.

5. **Personalize.** As you can see, the process of pondering and picturing leads to personalizing the passage and making it practical. There's an application in every verse to your life and mine. When we put our name on a promise of Scripture and stand on its truth, we've found a great antidote for alarm and anxiety.

6. **Pray.** We can also pray the scripture: "Lord, You have said my help comes from You, the Creator of the soaring hills. Now, here are areas in which I need Your help today . . ."

7. **Practice.** Then you put the passage into practice by trusting and obeying. Psalm 121 ends with the words, "The Lord shall preserve thy going out and thy coming in from this time forth, and even for evermore" (KJV). That's a great verse to keep in mind as I head out the door to work, or as I return home after a demanding day. I want to practice the awareness of God's watchful care over all my steps.

8. **Preach.** Sooner or later, you'll have an opportunity to preach the passage to others from whatever "pulpit" you have. Remember how I had an opportunity

to quote Philippians 4:4–9 to the woman on the plane? The words God gives us become, as it were, our own personal passages and our greatest treasures. We can't help sharing them with our children, friends, family, and with those we meet during the day.

The most powerful way of conducting family devotions, for example, is to naturally share with your children the verses that are currently enriching your life. Deuteronomy 6:6–7 says, "These commandments that I give you today are to be on your hearts. Impress them on your children. Talk about them when you sit at home and when you walk along the road, when you lie down and when you get up."

So that's my formula for meditation: Passage, Probe, Ponder, Paint, Personalize, Pray, Practice, Preach. If you want a simpler scheme, here's one I learned in college. The practice of meditation involves taking a passage of Scripture and *memorizing* it, *visualizing* it, and *personalizing* it. As you do this, your mind is healed by the transforming truth of God's Word and you begin increasingly to think the way God Himself thinks. You begin to look at life from God's point of view. You develop the wisdom from above (James 3:17).[7]

We should constantly have Scripture flowing through

our minds like water through a fountain or oil through a machine. One day while teaching at Liberty University, I had a wonderful conversation about this with my friend Dr. Gary Mathena. He told me of an experience involving his father, and I asked him if I could close this chapter with his story:

One of my dad's heroes in the ministry was an African-American preacher named Manuel Scott. After hearing Dr. Scott preach one evening, my dad had the opportunity to have breakfast with him the next day. As a young preacher, my dad expressed to Dr. Scott how much he was blessed, encouraged, and inspired by his preaching and the truths he was able to extrapolate out of the scripture. My dad said, "Dr. Scott, it is so evident that you are a spiritual man. How does a man become spiritual? How can I learn to preach with the insights and depth with which you preach?"

Manuel Scott thought for a moment and said, "Well, Harold, when you wake up in the morning, spend time reading and thinking about the Word of God and then, throughout the day, meditate and ruminate on the Word of God all day long. And then before you go to sleep at night, allow the Word of God to bathe your heart and mind." Then Dr. Scott paused and reached up to put his thumbs under his red suspenders and said, "If you'll do that, then one of these days, you'll just wake up spiritual!"[8]

That's the simplest way I know to convey the reality of thinking according to Scripture. If you want to calm your anxiety, start putting God's words, God's thoughts, and God's promises into your life and mind immediately. For as you think, so shall you be.

CHAPTER 6

The Habit of Influence

Some years ago, a Norwegian woman named Marie Monsen was among two hundred passengers traveling by ship across the Yellow Sea off the coast of China. During the wee hours of the morning she heard gunfire and the sounds of conflict. People shouting. Men arguing. Stampeding footsteps. A band of more than fifty pirates seized control of the ship, intent on holding the passengers as hostages.

Marie later described the thoughts that flashed to mind as she realized what was happening:

Just before daylight I heard pistol shots all over the ship, and I knew immediately what we were in for. The words came to me: "This is a trial of your faith." I remember the thrill of joy that went through me at the thought of it. I was immediately reminded of the word that I had

been using much in years gone by, in Isaiah 41:10, . . .
as I had been reading it down on the Honan plains,
"Fear not, Marie, for I am with thee; be not dismayed,
Marie, for I am thy God; I will strengthen thee, Marie,
yea, I will uphold thee, Marie, with the right hand of My
righteousness."[1]

Marie Monsen had been doing what I prescribed in
the last chapter—memorizing and personalizing key
passages of Scripture, in this case Isaiah 41:10—and the
Holy Spirit brought that verse instantly to her mind. For
twenty-three days, she stood on that promise. As she later
told the story, the pirates tried to intimidate her, but she
wasn't easily unnerved.

When they aimed their pistols at her, she told them no
weapon formed against her would succeed.

When they ordered her into the hold of the ship, she
refused to go.

When they told her to leave her cabin, she told them
God had given her that cabin and she wasn't leaving.

When one pirate stole her wristwatch, another
returned to it her.[2]

Her cabin was situated between the hijackers' head-
quarters and the ammunition store, so she had a bird's-eye
view of the action as the outlaws used the ship to inter-
cept and raid other vessels, but Marie never lost her sense
of peace. Nor was she averse to quoting Scripture to her

captors. For three weeks, she took every opportunity of sharing Christ with the passengers and pirates, including the chief, with whom she spent two hours explaining the gospel. Marie was finally released without suffering any harm. The pirates just didn't know what to do with a woman like her.[3]

When I read stories of people like Marie Monsen, I'm inspired to be more like them. They are true influencers in my life. If they trusted Christ in every situation, why shouldn't I? If they found courage in the Lord, so should I! It's humbling to put myself in their places and imagine how differently I might have reacted. I reckon I would have been fearful, panicked, and agitated, but maybe not. The lives of believers through the ages have taught us that God imparts grace as we need it, and there's nothing like having worthy models to follow, great mentors to emulate, and heroes to pave the way.

When the writer of the book of Hebrews wanted to encourage his nervous readers to persevere under pressure, he told them, "Now faith is confidence in what we hope for and assurance about what we do not see. This is what the ancients were commended for" (11:1–2). He then listed the examples of Abel, Enoch, Noah, Abraham, and the roll call of Old Testament heroes, who, through faith, conquered kingdoms, shut the mouths of lions, and gained what was promised.

We have two thousand more years of Christian

biography to add to that procession, and learning from their examples will strengthen our faith to overcome the armies of anxiety arrayed against us. If these men and women overcame fear, pulled down strongholds, lived boldly for their faith, and gained the reward, so can we. So can our generation.

They of course didn't consider themselves influencers, but they were all disciples. The word *disciple* literally means "learner," and it has to do with following and emulating the teaching and example of another. If we belong to Christ, we're primarily His disciples, but He often uses certain people to spur us on and instruct us, influencing and inspiring us in the truths and techniques of our faith. Some of these mentors dwell in yesteryear and cast their shadows over our pathways from afar. Others step right onto our pathway now and come alongside as friends, pastors, counselors, and teachers. We cannot overcome the anxieties of life without the help of these God-given allies.

This is a lifelong process. Even at so-called retirement age, I need mentors and advisers more than ever. We seldom evolve from anxious fear to unshakable faith overnight, but we can move from weakness to strength by persevering over time, especially when we let others help us. At one point, Paul encouraged his readers by telling them he was confident that the One "who began a good work in you will carry it on to completion until the day of

Christ Jesus" (Philippians 1:6). That involves process and progress.

The psalmist prayed, "The LORD will perfect that which concerns me; Your mercy, O LORD, endures forever" (Psalm 138:8 NKJV), or, as *The Message* puts it, "Finish what you started in me, God. Your love is eternal—don't quit on me now."

He won't quit on us, and we must not quit either. Month by month, year by year, and decade by decade, we can have greater calmness and composure, growing as sturdy as oaks with the passing of the seasons. Our anxious nerves can learn to relax in His love, lean on His promises, and trust in His grace. Our peace of mind can overwhelm the baser elements of our personalities. Someone said, "The older you get, the more you become like the place you're going." In Christ, we're headed to an unshakable city prepared for unsinkable souls, so we should learn from others how to be stronger during the journey.

True, we may have regressions along the way. Everyone who battles some variation of traumatic stress knows how our deepest fears can ignite in an instant when triggered by some word, event, sound, smell, or thought. But Proverbs 24:16 says, "The godly may trip seven times, but they will get up again. But one disaster is enough to overthrow the wicked" (NLT). With the examples of Jesus and His followers through all the ages, we have the resources to keep getting up, continuing on, and gaining ground until the Lord takes us home.

INFLUENCED BY THEIR EXAMPLES

A biblical practice that has helped me will help you too: if you're battling anxiety, find people who know how to trust the Lord better than you, and study their lives. Ask them about faith. Read their stories. Be discipled and influenced by their examples. In effect, their lives call out to us as the lives of the apostles and prophets did among the people in Scripture.

Naomi counseled Ruth, teaching her to wait and to rest in the guidance of the Lord. Elijah helped prepare Elisha for his life of service, as Elizabeth did for Mary of Nazareth. Samuel influenced David, and Jesus told His disciples, "Follow Me."

Paul wrote, "Join together in following my example, brothers and sisters, and just as you have us as a model, keep your eyes on those who live as we do" (Philippians 3:17). He said something similar in 1 Corinthians 11:1: "Follow my example, as I follow the example of Christ."

That sounds a little audacious, but we have to remember that the ancient Christians didn't have the full Bible like we do, and the Gentile converts of the New Testament knew little of the Old Testament. (Imagine being a convert in a newly established church, but having no Bible to study!) The great Handbook of Holiness, the New Testament, was still under construction. Perhaps some of the earliest New Testament writings like James and Galatians were beginning to circulate, and maybe one or two of Paul's letters as well, but they weren't widespread or readily available. So converts coming in waves across the Roman Empire had few documents to show them how Christians think, act, speak, or live. These first Christians wanted to know: How is a disciple of Christ different from everyone else?

While they didn't have the Bible in print, they did have the biblical culture embodied in the personalities of Paul, Peter, James, John, and the surviving apostolic band. The original followers of Christ exemplified and personified the Christian lifestyle, saying in effect, "If you want to live as a disciple, then watch us. Do what we do. Talk like we talk. Act like we act. Think like we think. Live like we live. Die like we die. Follow our example as we follow Christ. Whatever you have learned or received or heard from us, or seen in us—put it into practice. And the God of peace will be with you."

That statement about God's peace is a direct quote from Paul (Philippians 4:9). We have to remember how Paul had learned this peace. He wasn't seeing a therapist each week. He didn't have anti-anxiety meds he could take. He was living proof of the anxiety-fighting power of faith and its daily disciplines. Consequently, he was able to assure other Christians, especially those who were anxious or suffering, that God's peace is possible anywhere, any time. It can reach us and calm us in every situation.

Today we have the Bible—both the Old and New Testaments. We have the Gospel accounts and the letters and narratives and revelations. Yet we still need models and mentors—influencers—to help us see how the Word becomes flesh. We need patterns to follow.

If you study the greatest figures in Christian history, you'll always find a mentor behind them. The history of Christianity is the story of disciples mentoring and inspiring disciples, from generation to generation, from one era to the next, in an endless chain of transformation (2 Timothy 2:2).

When he was a young man, for example, Martin Luther had a mentor named Johann von Staupitz, the leader of the Augustinian community in Munich. Luther was an anxious and conflicted young monk, but von Staupitz taught him to look to Christ and wait on God's grace through prayer, not striving in his own efforts. Von Staupitz prompted Luther to study the book of Romans—a suggestion that changed history. What Luther realized through Romans both changed and emboldened him, and the Protestant Reformation was born.

Consider the statesman William Wilberforce, whose lifelong campaign against human trafficking ended commercial slavery in the British Empire. As a child, Wilberforce listened to the sermons of John Newton, the author of the hymn "Amazing Grace." Newton had been the captain of a slave ship before his conversion to Christ. Now he was a pastor and a great opponent of slavery.

The course of circumstances moved Wilberforce away from Newton's influence, and, as a teenager and young adult, the future statesman didn't have a strong Christian presence in his life. Indeed, he himself was not a Christian. But after being elected to Parliament at age twenty-one, Wilberforce was dramatically converted to Christ and wavered about staying in politics. He worried that the political world wasn't compatible with Christian values. He sought out his old pastor, John Newton, who encouraged him to remain in the government to advance the cause of Christ in the political arena and to strive for the abolition of slavery.

In the years that followed, many people vilified Wilberforce, and he often became anxious and stressed. At such times, he would confide in his mentor. On July 21, 1796, for example, Wilberforce wrote to Newton, disclosing his thoughts of retiring from public life. Newton wrote back:

> You meet with many things which weary and disgust you, which you would avoid in a more private life. But then they are inseparably connected with your path of duty; and though you cannot do all the good you wish for,

some good is done, and some evil is probably prevented by your influence. . . .

Nor is it possible at present to calculate all the advantages that may result from your having a seat in the House at such a time as this. The example, and even the presence of a consistent character may have a powerful, though unobserved, effect upon others. You are not only a representative for Yorkshire, you have the far greater honour of being a representative for the Lord, in a place where many know Him not.[4]

Newton ended his letter by reminding Wilberforce of the example of the statesman and prophet Daniel who served in the courts of Babylon:

It is true that you live in the midst of difficulties and snares, and you need a double guard of watchfulness and prayer. But since you know both your need of help, and where to look for it, I may say to you as Darius to Daniel, "Thy God whom thou servest continually is able to preserve and deliver you." Daniel, likewise, was a public man, and in critical circumstances; but he trusted in the Lord, was faithful in his department, and therefore, though he had enemies, they could not prevail against him.

Indeed the great point for our comfort in life is to have a well grounded persuasion that we are where, all things considered, we ought to be.[5]

Notice how John Newton mentored Wilberforce back to the biblical model of Daniel, and in so doing gave him an example of a man who, in similar governmental straits, kept calm and carried on. We, too, can learn to withstand the pressures of anxiety by looking to biblical models, examples in Christian biography, and contemporary friends and mentors whose lives show us how to better trust the Lord. In other words, if you're beset by anxiety, find someone who isn't and learn their secret.

FOUR GREAT WAYS OF BEING INFLUENCED

In the Bible we find four main ways our mentors instruct and influence us: through what we learn, receive, hear, or see from them.

The Life-Changing Lessons You Learn

The learning you gain refers to the *life-changing lessons* God teaches through those He sends across your path. As I reflect on my life, I'm grateful for fellow believers who have modeled biblical truth for me and taught me the principles of Scripture—my parents, my childhood pastor Winford R. Floyd, my professors, a handful of upperclassmen at Columbia International University, and a band of brothers and sisters God has brought into my life along the way.

In our book *The Strength You Need*, my wife, Katrina, wrote about the woman who mentored her in Palm

Beach, Florida: Antoinette Johnson. Her influence shaped Katrina's life and set her on a new course of growth—without which she and I would never have met.

And speaking of Katrina, no one has helped me more than she in grappling with my anxieties. "I don't know why you're so worried," she has often told me. "You act as though God can't do anything about this. Why don't you just trust Him?"

"I'm trying to trust," I sometimes say.

"*Trying* and *trusting* are opposites," is her invariable response.

These are life-changing lessons of faith we can learn from others.

Whatever your age or stage in life, God has blessed you with someone—or soon will—who can mentor you from a life of anxious care into a life of productive peace. You may be new to faith, new to your job—or you may be a longtime Christian in a position of leadership. No matter who you are, God can bring you a humble influencer who can take you deeper into the life of faith with life-changing lessons.

Ian Maclaren wrote of a church in Drumtochty, Ireland, where a young John Carmichael had just begun his ministry. Carmichael worked hard on his sermons, but Sunday after Sunday they fell apart as he tried to preach them.

One Sunday after the service when everyone had left, Carmichael remained in the church, feeling dejected. He was sitting alone in the vestry, chin on his chest, when he heard a knock at the door. It was the most senior elder in the church, Angus Sutherland. John braced himself, thinking he was about to be discharged.

"It is good weather we're having, sir," Angus began, speaking English with a soft Scottish accent. "Maybe I should not be troubling you at this time, but I have been sent by the elders with a message."

Then old Angus said, "It has been three months since you entered upon your ministry among us, and you will not be angry with me if I am saying to you that you are very young to have so heavy a weight upon you, for there is no burden like the burden for souls." He went on to say no one doubted the young man's sincerity or his hard efforts. "But you are very young and the ministry of the Lord is very arduous."

He paused before continuing: "So the elders considered that the full time had come for their saying something to you, and I was charged by them all to . . . say unto you, on behalf of the elders of the flock and all the flock which is under your care, that we are all thankful unto God that He sent you to be our minister, and are all full of wonder at the treasures of truth and grace which you will be bringing to us every Sabbath."

He added:

There is just one other thing that the brethren laid upon me to say. We will ask you to remember when you stand

in your place to speak to us in the name of the Lord, that
as the smoke goeth up from the homes of the people in
the morning, so will their prayers be ascending for their
minister; and as you look down upon us before you begin
to speak, maybe you will say to yourself, next Sabbath,
they are all loving me. Oh, yes, and it will be true from
the oldest to the youngest, we will all be loving you very
much.[6]

No wonder John Carmichael remained in the ministry all his life. The lesson he learned from his elder that
Sunday afternoon helped him conquer his nerves, overcome his fears, and persevere in the work for a lifetime.

The Life-Changing Writings You Receive

We're also mentored into peace by *life-changing
writings*. It's possible to read our way to greater peace of
mind if we read the right books (starting with the Bible of
course). In the words we read, the sages of the ages become
our mentors.

Sometimes when I open a book, even in the deepest of night, I feel I'm entertaining its author, whether
Augustine, John Bunyan, Thomas Watson, Brother
Lawrence, Charles Spurgeon, A. W. Tozer, or C. S. Lewis.
We've had wonderful times together, and some of these
influencers and their wisdom have changed my life, my
thinking, and my attitudes. They've empowered me to

grow in my faith and to better cope with my anxieties. You might call it biblio-therapy.

I never met Charles Spurgeon; he died sixty years before I was born. But his *Lectures to My Students* crossed my path, and I became Spurgeon's student through his book.

I've never met Chattanooga psychologist Ross Campbell, but his book *How to Really Love Your Child* helped me be a better parent.

J. I. Packer's *Knowing God* became one of the greatest forces influencing my generation, and I still keep a copy on the shelf by my desk. Some of the truths in *that book* have seeped by natural osmosis into this one. That's just what happens with great writings—they soak into our minds and are diffused into our conversations and writings.

When it comes to worry and anxiety, a couple of recent biographies have put things into perspective for me. In *God's Hostage*, Andrew Brunson wrote about learning to trust God during his 735 days of Turkish persecution and imprisonment. And in *Imprisoned with ISIS*, Petr Jasek told a similar story of his 445 days of persecution and imprisonment in Sudan. I couldn't put either book down, and the stories helped me by showing me how these men of faith had struggled and triumphed in unspeakable conditions.

I'd love to have dinner with both men, with some more

dinners scheduled with the likes of Tim Keller, Randy Acorn, Os Guinness, and Anne Graham Lotz.

Even from a distance, these writers encourage me!

The Life-Changing Teachings You Hear

There is electrifying power in the *life-changing teachings* you hear, starting with the public reading and exposition of God's Word through sermons, to the lectures and broadcasts and podcasts you listen to.

When I was a freshman in college, I was very immature and lukewarm in my faith. But I happened to turn on the radio while visiting my aunt Louise in North Carolina, and it was tuned to a station that would broadcast a sermon each night from a Bible conference somewhere in the country. That evening, a British speaker was preaching about the donkey Jesus rode into Jerusalem. That donkey was made for a purpose, said the preacher, and it was standing in a place where two ways met: in the right place and at the right time. Jesus needed that little donkey, and the animal fulfilled its destiny by serving the Lord. "If God can do something with that donkey," explained the speaker, "maybe He can do something with you."

That preacher might as well have jumped through the radio and grabbed me by the collar. I felt he was talking personally to me. That was my first step on the road to yielding my life to the Lord in full surrender.

In college, it was the lectures of James (Buck) Hatch

that laid the foundation for my whole approach to understanding and teaching the Bible. Truth be told, I still go back and listen to his recorded lectures, which I first heard fifty years ago.[7]

There's a thought blowing like a stray leaf through church auditoriums today that the most effective sermons are those with the least Scripture. Some preachers habitually preach on the moral or practical themes of Scripture while avoiding digressions into what the Bible actually says. But Psalm 119:130 says, "The unfolding of your words gives light." The act of preaching or teaching isn't simply proclaiming our thoughts about God's Word. It's the act of unfolding the words themselves, preaching Scripture progressively, verse by verse, in a way that reflects the logic God wove into the Bible.

When you find a solid Bible expositor, read and study his or her scriptural insights, for as you understand the unfolding logic of God's Word, you'll be better armed to deal with life's perils and alarms.

The Life-Giving Examples You See

Paul said, "Whatever you have . . . *seen* in me—put it into practice. And the God of peace will be with you" (Philippians 4:9). This brings us full circle to the *life-giving examples* that strengthen our faith and reduce our fear as we observe them. Some in the first century never sat down and talked with the apostle Paul. Some never read his letters. Perhaps they didn't have a chance to hear him teach or preach. But they watched him from afar, and he was able to influence them without speaking a word. They saw the disciplines in his life. They saw the hope in his eyes. They heard about his enthusiasm even amid suffering, and they understood he wasn't a man easily rattled. His life was anchored to hope in Christ. "And because of my chains," he said, "most of the brothers and sisters have become confident in the Lord and dare all the more to proclaim the gospel without fear" (Philippians 1:14).

The very presence of people of faith has enormous impact on those who cross their paths. One of the women I wish I'd met was Dr. Henrietta Mears, who served on the staff of a California church in the 1940s, but whose ministry covered the world and whose influence touched countless lives over the years. In his book on revival, Bill Bright talked about a life-changing evening in 1947. He said:

> I was in a meeting at Forest Home Christian Conference in California. A dear friend of mine, Dr. Henrietta Mears, director of Christian education at the First Presbyterian Church of Hollywood, was the speaker. Dr. Louis Evans Jr., the son of the senior pastor, and I walked her back to her cabin. We were chatting and enjoying our fellowship, so she invited us in. As we continued to talk, suddenly the Holy Spirit enveloped us. As a young believer, I did

not know very much about the person of the Holy Spirit, so I did not know what was happening to me. But I found myself intoxicated with joy. Dr. Evans said it was as though coals of fire ran up and down his spine.

While we were in prayer and praising God, Dr. Richard Halverson entered Dr. Mears's cabin. He was a defeated, frustrated, fruitless Presbyterian minister from Coalinga, California. He had come to seek her counsel on how he might leave the ministry and return to the Hollywood entertainment world from which he had come before his conversion.

When he walked into the room, we were praying and no one said anything to him. But instantly the Holy Spirit healed him of his defeat and frustration, and his heart was filled with joy and love.

In moments we were all changed. None of us was ever the same again, and God gave each of us major responsibilities in His vineyard. Dr. Evans went on to become a nationally-known Presbyterian minister. For many years he pastored the National Presbyterian Church, "the church of the presidents." Dr. Halverson became chaplain of the U.S. Senate.[8]

And Bill Bright? He went on to establish Campus Crusade for Christ, now known as Cru, which became one of the greatest evangelistic forces of the twentieth century, one that still continues in 191 countries.

Henrietta Mears didn't cause that moment of revival in her cabin; the Holy Spirit did. As I've read her biographies, however, I've noticed that moments like that seemed to happen when she was around. Oh, how we want our own lives to radiate revival and to encourage others to wait upon the Lord, to mount up with wings like eagles, and to overcome the lower climates of fear, worry, anxiety, discouragement, and defeat.

To seek out Christian influencers—those disciples throughout history who have devoted themselves to following Him—is a habit that revamps us into replicas of Christ, whose peace transcends understanding. Whatever you have learned or received or heard or seen from others that is worthy of Him, put it into practice.

In order to bury your anxiety before it buries you, look around you. Find someone else with a shovel in their hand, who, by faith, is already putting their anxious cares six feet under. Someone whose face reflects the peace you need. It may be a friend, a grandparent, a writer, a pastor, a coach, or a senior saint. Get to know them. Learn from them. Talk with them if possible and ask, "How did you learn to trust the Lord as you do?"

And as you follow their example, you'll begin to notice others looking to you for some added strength in their own lives. And you can tell them, "Whatever you have learned or received or heard from me, or seen in me—put it into practice. And the God of peace will be with you."

This is the habit of influence at its best.

CHAPTER 7

The Habit of Gentleness

Richard and Arline Baughman were married in 1940, just before America entered World War II. Richard was drafted in 1942, and left for the war just a few weeks after the birth of their first son. For more than a year he was unable to communicate much with his family, and when he returned to his Wisconsin home, he bore the scars of posttraumatic stress from combat experiences. He had a lot of bad dreams. But he and Arline picked up where they left off, and in the years until her death in 2017, they faced everything together. Richard worked as a mail carrier and farmer. Arline was a schoolteacher. They lived a busy life and raised six children, one of whom passed away. Over the years the Baughmans encountered all the stresses and strains that come with life, just like you and me.

But here's what set them apart. A little over a year before

Arline's passing, this couple celebrated their seventy-fifth anniversary. Richard was ninety-seven and Arline was ninety-six years old at the time. Somehow their story got out, and they were in the news—especially because of an almost unbelievable part of their testimony. In seventy-five years of marriage, they said, they had never had a single argument. Not one. "If we had differences we just talked about it," they said. "We didn't have dishes to throw or shoes to throw because we couldn't afford it. So, we had to get along."[1]

They explained that whenever they felt angry they would give themselves time to cool off before talking it through, and they've always taken time for regular dates and for occasional trips and vacations. They've worked hard, lived simply, and have tried not to complain to each other. "The couple's advice for a happy marriage," said a reporter who interviewed them, "is to not fret over the small things and to keep faith in the Lord alive."[2]

To me, that's the living embodiment of the spiritual fruit that the Bible refers to as gentleness (Galatians 5:23). A gentle spirit is a direct by-product of a relationship with Christ. At the same time, as we're about to see, cultivating a more patient, gentler personality is a great way to lower the stresses of life.

This may surprise you as a foundational habit for easing our anxiety, but God's Word reminds each of us that, "if it is possible, as far as it depends on you, live at peace with everyone" (Romans 12:18). As often as we can, we need to get along with each other, and "getting along" relationally means exhibiting a spirit of gentleness.

WHAT IS GENTLENESS?

When I looked up *gentle* in the dictionary, I was surprised to find the primary definitions were in the negative. The dictionary talked about what gentleness is not. *Gentleness*, said various dictionaries, means *not* severe, *not* rough, *not* violent. It refers to the *absence of* a bad temper or of belligerence. People who are gentle are *not* harsh, irritable, petulant, or easily offended.

Of course, we can't simply define something by what it's not. This is a positive-sounding word, and we can begin to ferret out a positive definition for gentleness by checking the origin of the English term. The opening syllable—*gen*—comes from the same Latin term that gives us *Genesis, genetics, generation,* and *genital.* It has to do with begetting a family or being part of the same lineage or clan. The word *gentle* originally had to do with the way a mother or father would treat a newborn and with the way we should feel toward those we most love, who are part of our own family.

From its Latin origin, the term passed into the French language, where the Old French version was *gentil*, which meant "born into a good family, highborn, noble." From there it came into our English language as *genteel* ("well-bred, belonging to a polite society") and *gentle* ("moderate, tender, and kind"). Over time, *gentleness* came to imply softness, a pleasant demeanor, a naturally sympathetic outlook, or the absence of sharp edges to one's personality. Gentleness suggests a deliberate or voluntary kindness or forbearance in dealing with others. Gentle people are amiable, considerate, pleasant, and well-tempered. Various English translations of the Bible have rendered this word "considerate," "reasonable," and "gracious."

I looked up all twenty-three occurrences of the word *gentle* in the Bible, and based on those references I want to suggest my own definition. When Scripture talks about gentleness, it refers to "the ability to stay calm in all our conflicts and kind in all our conduct."

It doesn't mean weakness. It means that in any given situation we've developed the inner resources to remain as calm and kind as is possible under the circumstances. That's one of the greatest assets we can possess. It's a supernatural quality and a spiritual temper of soul. It is Jesus living through us, because we're not like that on our own, and it's vital to developing a Christian personality.

Think of your interactions with your children, your spouse, your coworkers, the baristas at coffee shops, the clerks behind the counters at discount stores, and even the nuisance callers on the phone. Are you consistently pleasant, calm, and kind?

Yes, there are times to be abrupt and adamant. There are moments to draw a line, to stand up for ourselves, to argue a point, to establish boundaries, and to remain true to what's right. Yet we should always do so as gently as possible in any given circumstance. There is never a moment when we should be one degree harsher than we must. We should always be as gentle as possible, and our gentleness should manifest itself in our eyes, in our facial expression, in our body posture, in the tone of our voices, and in our subsequent actions.

As I studied the occurrences of the word *gentle* in the Bible, I came away with four great benefits that come into the lives of gentle people.

REDUCES ANXIETY

First, a gentle spirit reduces anxiety. When you read between the lines of Scripture, you get the idea that some of its personalities had rough edges. As we know from the New Testament epistles, some of the churches were exemplary, but not perfect. Apparently, some of the pews were occupied by people who had sharp angles to their temperaments.

That's true almost anywhere we go. We've all known somebody at work or school or in the neighborhood who likes to stir up drama. Or we've encountered that person online who can't ever refrain from making mean comments. But all too often, we find those rough-edged folks closer to home.

As the mother of my friend Keith Fletcher grew older, she became increasingly cantankerous, difficult, and critical. Her sharp remarks made her a bit of a challenge to live with. A couple of months after she passed away, Keith had a dream about her. He dreamed he came downstairs for supper and there she was sitting at the table, the same as always.

"Mom! You're here!" Keith exclaimed. "You're back."

She nodded.

"But you passed away and went to heaven," he said.

She nodded again.

"Mom, if you've been to heaven, you've seen it and you can tell us all about it. What's it like there? What is heaven really like?"

She shot a glance at him and said curtly, "I didn't like it!"

The real question isn't whether we know people like that. It's whether we're like that ourselves more often than we realize. Keith's mother reflects our own natural tendencies. It's all too easy to be like her. Just last week while reading in the book of Numbers during my morning devotions, I was struck by the critical attitudes of the children of Israel in the desert. Their constant complaining resembled smokestacks billowing out smog at full blast, and I grew convicted about my own tendency to grumble and whine about my workload, my fatigue, my busyness, my aches and pains, and all the rest of it.

Gentle people learn to temper their attitudes with a pleasant, patient approach that's quietly adjusted and recalibrated every day during their devotions. In his book *Breakfast with Fred*, management consultant Fred Smith told of his friend Ron Glosser, who was the head of the Hershey Trust Company in Hershey, Pennsylvania. Glosser said that when he found himself being overly critical, the problem was likely to be in his own heart rather than in the other person's behavior. Glosser realized he needed a way to keep his thinking healthy. He said, "I have found that the best way to keep from being overly critical is to get myself centered early in the day. For me, this is achieved by reading the Scriptures and praying. I try to identify myself as the beloved child of God and to see all those with whom I come in contact that same way."[3]

When we fail to do this, we face needless tension. Some people keep everyone torn up. They are always involved in conflict and raise stress levels wherever they go. Difficult or demanding people put a lot of pressure on themselves and others. The Bible is full of examples of those whose lives were complicated by a stern or stubborn demeanor.

- In 1 Samuel 25, a wealthy farmer named Nabal had the reputation of being surly and rude in his dealings.

He got into an altercation with David and his men, and he ended up having a stroke and dying.

- In 1 Kings 12, King Rehoboam entertained a delegation of countrymen asking him to relax governmental policies. Rehoboam consulted his older advisers, who counseled him to listen to the people and respond with gentleness and favor. The king then sought the advice of the buddies he had grown up with, and they suggested a harsh approach. Rehoboam took a rigid stand against his people. As a result, he lost ten of the twelve tribes that made up his kingdom. The nation of Israel split apart like a ripped sheet and was never reunified.

- In the New Testament, Paul dealt with many difficult people, and on one occasion he cautioned Titus about being drawn into conflicts with such people. He said, "Warn a divisive person once, and then warn them a second time. After that, have nothing to do with them. You may be sure that such people are warped and sinful; they are self-condemned" (Titus 3:10–11).

Based on what we read in Scripture, it doesn't take a social-science degree to make a simple observation: Some people create anxiety for themselves and for others by disagreeableness, by their sharp tongues, by their opinionated personalities, and by their irritable spirits. When you're upset, you upset others, which piles on layers of stress like wet blankets. If you're angry at home, you'll upset your marriage. If you're harsh at work, you'll have more conflicts.

To reduce anxiety, then, develop a gentle spirit.

In one of her uplifting poems, Helen Steiner Rice put it like this:

> At the spot God placed you
> Begin at once to do
> Little things that brighten up
> The lives surrounding you.
> For if everybody brightened up
> The spot on which they're standing
> By being more considerate
> And a little less demanding
> This dark old world would very soon
> Eclipse the "Evening Star"
> If everybody brightened up
> The corner where they are.[4]

REFLECTS CHRIST

A gentle spirit not only reduces anxiety, it also reflects Christ. In Matthew 11:29, Jesus spoke of Himself as "gentle and humble in heart," and in Matthew 21:5, others described Him as being "gentle and riding on a . . . colt."

This didn't keep Jesus from speaking plainly when necessary. There were times He condemned hypocrites, denounced cities, and rebuked demons. He occasionally spoke sharply (Matthew 16:23), and just a reproachful glance could reduce a grown man to tears (Luke 22:61–62). But there was never a time when Jesus lost control of Himself or of His words or emotions. The default setting on His personality was one of compassion, love, gentleness, patience, and humility—a willingness to touch and help those with whom He came in contact.

I have a small ornamental pond along the front corner of my house, and several years ago I purchased two small koi fish. I paid six or seven dollars each for them, and they grew very quickly. But they were so skittish we had trouble seeing them. From a distance we could see them swimming around in their little world, but as soon as we would approach, they'd panic as if we were going to kill and eat them. They'd dart back and forth, desperately looking for a rock or lily pad to hide behind. I read many articles about how to tame koi, but we never really were able to establish fellowship.

That resembles how we sometimes feel toward God. He rises up, towers over us, and gazes down into our little pond, and we're afraid of Him. He is vast, unbounded, absolute in all His attributes and holy in all His ways. In one respect, the proper fear of the Lord represents a healthy attitude of reverence and awe. But our Lord is also a loving God, and He did the unimaginable by jumping into the pond with us, as it were. When we see Jesus, we see the gentleness and the tenderness and the compassion of God, and according to Hosea 11:4, the Lord draws us to Himself with "gentle cords, with bands of love" (NKJV).

Sometimes when I feel particularly sinful or unworthy, I think of the verse that is spoken about Christ in both the Old and the New Testaments: "A bruised reed he will not break, and a smoldering wick he will not snuff out" (Isaiah 42:3; Matthew 12:20).

God loves you and me greatly and gently, and through Jesus Christ, He reaches out to us with all the tenderness of His nail-scarred hands. When we respond to His love and receive Him as Lord and Savior, He moves into our hearts and begins to remodel our temperaments. He permeates our personalities with nine different attitudes, which reflect His own character. These are called the "fruit of the Spirit," and as I mentioned at the beginning of this chapter, one of them is gentleness. Galatians 5:19–23 says, "The acts of the flesh are obvious . . . hatred, discord, jealously, fits of rage, selfish ambition, dissensions, factions. . . . But the fruit of the Spirit is love, joy, peace, forbearance, kindness, goodness, faithfulness, gentleness and self-control."

Another passage along the same lines, Ephesians 4:1–2, says, "Live a life worthy of the calling you have received. Be completely humble and gentle." In other words, when we are completely humble and completely gentle, we demonstrate a life worthy of the calling we have received.

Husbands and wives need to remember this in their marriages, and parents need to practice this with their children. Brothers and sisters need to remember this. Many of our most anxious or stressful moments occur within family relationships, often under the same roof. We feel neglected or affronted. We get angry. We argue. We speak harshly. We insult. We yell or scream. We lose our temper and our compassion. We sulk and withdraw our love. None of that reflects the personality of the Lord Jesus Christ.

In her book *I Never Walk the Halls Alone*, Donna Kincheloe wrote about her experiences as a critical-care nurse. One of her most touching memories involved her grandfather, who had raised her. When she received word of his heart attack, she raced to his side in a Pennsylvania hospital, where she found him unable to speak. He tried desperately to communicate, but he couldn't vocalize his words. Through long experience in intensive care units, Donna had learned to read lips and she quickly realized her grandfather was pleading to see his two children, Dee and Bud. Years before, these two siblings had argued and grown embittered toward each other. They had not spoken for a dozen years. Now they met at their dying father's bedside.

"My mom and Uncle Bud wanted me there to interpret, so, next visiting time, the three of us went to

Grandpa's bedside," Donna recalled. "Mom was on his left and Uncle Bud was on his right. Grandpa reached up and took Mom's right hand and Bud's left hand and put them together. He then covered their hands with his own strong mechanic's hands and mouthed two words over and over, 'Make up. Make up. Make up.'"[5]

Donna went on to suggest that Jesus, by His death, had a similar objective. He wants to reunite us with our heavenly Father and with each other, and His wounded hands can bring healing to our relationships and replace hostility with gentleness and understanding.[6]

That was Paul's message in Philippians 4 when he told church members Euodia and Syntyche to make up. He called on others to help the women through the process of healing, and he told the whole church to practice gentleness: "Let your gentleness be evident to all" (vv. 2–3, 5).

To the Colossian church he wrote,

As God's chosen people, holy and dearly loved, clothe yourselves with compassion, kindness, humility, gentleness and patience. Bear with each other and forgive one another if any of you has a grievance against someone. Forgive as the Lord forgave you. And over all these virtues put on love, which binds them all together in perfect unity.

Let the peace of Christ rule in your hearts, since as members of one body you were called to peace. And be thankful. (Colossians 3:12–15)

GETS THINGS DONE

As I studied the occurrences of the words *gentle* and *gentleness* in the Bible, I also ran into a pragmatic truth. The Bible says we should be gentle because gentleness gets things done. It works. It makes us more efficient, productive, and profitable in the daily business of life.

There are two verses about this in the book of Proverbs. The first is Proverbs 25:15: "Through patience a ruler can be persuaded, and a gentle tongue can break a bone." One of the softest parts of our body is the tongue. God created it with flexibility and motion so we can eat and speak. The most unyielding parts of our body are our bones, which are so rigid we can stand upright. But according to Proverbs 25:15, a gentle tongue is stronger than a rigid bone. We could paraphrase this verse to say that a person who knows how to speak gently will be more effective in any situation than someone who is rigid and severe. The New Century Version says, "A gentle word can get through to the hard-headed."

I learned this lesson when I was in high school and working at Jim Chambers Men's Shop in my hometown of Elizabethton, Tennessee. Jim was a wonderful man, a Christian, and he'd been a retailer for many years with a loyal base of customers in our community. One day while I was working in the back of the store, a man—a farmer and a hillbilly—burst into the store like a thunderclap. He was upset over a pair of shoes he had purchased. He let Jim have it, telling him how sorry the shoes were, how they hurt his feet, how they didn't fit right, how they weren't made well, how he'd been cheated. There in front of Jim and the other customers, he flew into a fit. My heart stopped and I felt a panic attack coming on. Jim just stood there, looking at the man and at the shoes and nodding thoughtfully during the rant.

When the man finished, I waited for my boss to let him have it. But Jim simply said, "Mr. Farmer, I'm sorry you don't like your shoes. Sometimes we just get a bad pair, don't we? What would you like me to do about it? Would you like your money back? Would you like another pair of shoes? I'll be glad to give you another pair. You just pick them out. Here, I'll throw in a pair of socks."

The farmer wilted. He looked down, his anger spent, and he said, "Well, I guess another pair of shoes would be all right, Jim."

Jim looked at me and said, "Robert, help this man find another pair of shoes." I guess Jim didn't know I panicked in confrontation, and my hands were shaking a bit as I pulled boxes off the shelves. But I got the farmer shod, and as soon as he was out the door, Jim smiled at me and said, "I lost a pair of shoes but I kept a customer."

That leads to the other great verse about this in Proverbs, one of the most psychologically sound verses of Scripture—Proverbs 15:1: "A gentle answer turns away wrath, but a harsh word stirs up anger." That's a verse to post to the bulletin board of your memory. It's a sentence to teach our children as soon as they're old enough to memorize it. It's only thirteen words, and most are one syllable. But no verse in the Bible conveys better psychology, or a better approach to people in our hyper-vocal, strongly opinionated, oppositional world.

Proverbs 15:1 also seeps into many other New Testament passages, which advise leaders to master the art of the gentle answer. The apostle Paul instructed Timothy to appoint church overseers who were "not violent but gentle, not quarrelsome" (1 Timothy 3:3).

A bit later, Paul added, "Do not rebuke an older man harshly, but exhort him as if he were your father. Treat younger men as brothers, older women as mothers, and younger women as sisters" (5:1–2). He went on to tell Timothy to cultivate certain leadership traits in his personality, including "righteousness, godliness, faith, love, endurance and gentleness" (6:11).

Paul instructed another protégé, Titus, to be "gentle toward everyone" and to teach all the church members to be the same (Titus 3:2).

The apostle Peter told us to adopt the same strategy, even with unbelievers who don't know Christ. "In your hearts revere Christ as Lord," wrote Peter. "Always be prepared to give an answer to everyone who asks you to give the reason for the hope that you have. But do this with gentleness and respect" (1 Peter 3:15).

Successful people cultivate the quality of gentleness, which means reining in the rougher elements of their tempers and practicing self-control with their tongues. They have learned to be calm in their conflict and kind in their conduct. With a little thought, we can devise personal techniques that allow our gentleness to show through too.

Rocky Forshey of Houston, Texas, told me that years ago when his children were young he would grow upset at them and tramp through the house to scold them. Passing a mirror once, he was shocked at the fierce countenance on his face. He realized that's how his children saw him. He instantly softened his face, and he took the lesson to heart. He began practicing relaxing his expression whenever he spoke with his children, and it became a lifelong habit that has given Rocky a gentler countenance that isn't rocky at all.[7]

John Wooden, one of the most revered coaches in the history of college basketball, credited much of his success to his dad. He recalled a boyhood occasion when he watched his father deal with a situation that needed a calmer solution.

Their rural Indiana county would pay local farmers to take teams of mules or horses into the local gravel pits and haul out loads of gravel. Some pits were deeper than others, and sometimes it was hard for a team to pull a wagon filled with gravel out through the wet sand and up the steep incline.

One steamy summer day, wrote Wooden, a young farmer was trying to get his team of plow horses to bring a fully loaded wagon out of the pit. He was whipping and cursing those beautiful animals, which were frothing at the mouth, stomping, and pulling back from him. The elder Wooden watched for a while, then went over to the young man and said, "Let me take 'em for you."

> Dad started talking to the horses, almost whispering to them, and stroking their noses with a soft touch. Then he walked between them, holding their bridles and bits while he continued talking—very calmly and gently—as they settled down. Gradually he stepped out in front of them and gave a little whistle to start them moving forward while he guided the reins. Within moments, those two big plow horses pulled the wagon out of the gravel pit as easy as could be. As if they were happy to do it.[8]

John Wooden said, "I've never forgotten what I saw him do and how he did it. Over the years I've seen a lot of leaders act like that angry young farmer who lost control. . . . So much more can usually be accomplished by Dad's calm, confident, and steady approach."[9]

Wooden took away an indelible lesson: "It takes strength inside to be gentle on the outside."[10]

Gentleness does not imply weakness; it conveys strength, maturity, self-control, and a desire to be productive in life. It requires a strong self-image. Insecure people get their dander up. They feel threatened. They feel slighted and offended, and they compensate by over-reacting. As we mature in Christ, we exchange our low image of ourselves with a high image of Christ. The Holy Spirit forms His personality within us and teaches us the incredible power of a gentle spirit.

PLEASES THE LORD

And that pleases the Lord, which brings me to my final thought. God is delighted when we are gentle, and He is grieved when we aren't. There's a wonderful verse about this in the Bible. It was originally addressed to women, but its message is transferable to all of us.

> Your beauty should not come from outward adornment, such as elaborate hairstyles and the wearing of gold jewelry or fine clothes. Rather, it should be that of your inner self, the unfading beauty of a gentle and quiet spirit, which is of great worth in God's sight. (1 Peter 3:3–4)

Look at those words: "a gentle . . . spirit, which is of great worth in God's sight." According to the apostle Peter, this is true elegance, and it's the way we make ourselves appealing to others, to the world, and to the Lord.

When I was a boy, my parents—both schoolteachers—sometimes took me to Knoxville, Tennessee, for their educational conferences, and we always stayed downtown at the Farragut Hotel, next door to the S&W Cafeteria. One year my elderly grandparents accompanied us, and during supper my grandfather, Clifton Palmer, grew agitated. Turning to my mom, he said, "An old man across the room keeps scowling at me." We all looked, of course. The opposite wall was lined with mirrors, and my grandfather had been looking at no one but himself.

If only we could see the expression on our faces the way others see us!

If you want a more attractive face, learn to be gentle, quiet, and confident in your demeanor. Ecclesiastes 8:1 says, "A person's wisdom brightens their face and changes its hard appearance." Gentleness is the world's most exclusive beauty secret. If only we could bottle it! It relaxes our faces and releases our smiles. It pleases God.

There's scant gentleness in our world. Just turn on the television or talk radio. Watch a movie. Read blog comments or social media posts. People are indignant. People are shouting at each other. People insult one another in our increasingly coarse culture. And between the pandemic and all the politics that came with it, it's only gotten worse. A demanding spirit has seeped into many homes and churches. Maybe our own homes and churches.

I confess I'm not as gentle as I should be in reacting to provocation or fatigue or stress. But as Christians we should be keen to improve. When we trust Jesus Christ as our Lord and Savior, we begin to change and we keep improving as long as we're on earth. And a gentle spirit reduces our stress, reflects Christ, gets things done, and pleases the Lord.

Remember what Saint Francis de Sales said: "Nothing is so strong as gentleness, nothing so gentle as real strength."[11] A good place to start is by putting gentleness into action.

CHAPTER 8

The Habit of Peace

T he inimitable Puritan writer Thomas Watson said, "If God be our God . . . He will give us peace in trouble. When there is a storm without, He will make music within. The world can create trouble in peace, but God can create peace in trouble."[1]

The Prince of Preachers agreed. In one of his matchless sermons, delivered on Sunday, August 3, 1890, Charles Spurgeon, age fifty-seven, who was celebrating his fortieth year as a Christian, told his congregation that if they had inner peace they would "dread no outward disturbance, and feel no inward storm—who does not desire such a state?"

His text that morning was Psalm 29:11: "The LORD blesses his people with peace." Waxing eloquent, Spurgeon spoke of the thoughts that had come into his mind the previous evening while meditating on this text:

As I turned my text over last night, it seemed to me to be a very wonderful passage. . . . "The Lord will bless His people with peace." We have had peace with God these forty years; yes, but we have a promise of peace for today. Suppose we should live another forty years, we shall still have the same promise—"The Lord will bless His people with peace."

I should like an everlasting check from some million-aire, running thus: "So often as this check is presented at the bank, pay the bearer what he asks." Few persons possessed of such a document would fail to put in an appearance at the bank. We should be regular visitors. Oh, children of God, we have such a promissory note in the text before you! The Lord hath endless, boundless peace within Himself, and when you have long enjoyed peace with Him you may go to Him again and say, "Lord, renew my peace. I am troubled, but Thou art unmoved. Bless me with peace."

When you are rich . . . when you are poor. . . . When children are born to you . . . if the children die. . . . If you grow sick. . . . When you must go upstairs and lie down upon your last bed to rise no more, then, even then, the Lord will bless you with His ever-living peace; and when you wake up at the sound of the last trump, the Lord will still keep you in perfect peace. . . . The Lord will bless His people with peace.

Take this truth home to your heart, and live upon

it, and you may dwell perpetually in the presence of the King.[2]

According to everything we've seen in Scripture, as we practice the habits that God has laid out for us, our susceptibility to surging worry will recede and we'll find ourselves facing the pressures of our problems with less panic and greater peace—transcendent peace.

On occasions that tempt us to feel anxious, we can take a deep breath, close our eyes a moment, and pray. We can rejoice in the Lord, and find reasons for giving thanks, and exercise gentleness. We can meditate on the Bible passages that resonate with us. The result is guaranteed. As we do these things consistently, the power of God's comforting Spirit and His holy words will overhaul our minds like an engineer renovating an engine, until all our thoughts, feelings, and reactions vibrate with peace. Somehow in His infinite grace, God reduces our fears and replaces them with a peace that transcends all understanding. Marvelous peace. Perfect peace. Multiplied peace.

MORE GRACE, MULTIPLIED PEACE

The concept of multiplied peace was a great encouragement to the disabled hymnist Annie Johnson Flint. Her classic poem "He Giveth More Grace" speaks of how God multiplies peace amid multiplied trials and how He gives more grace when our strength is low, when our resources are depleted, and when our labors increase. "He giveth, and giveth, and giveth again," she wrote.[3]

I have a friend—Karen Singer—whose uncle, Hubert Mitchell, set Annie Johnson Flint's poem "He Giveth More Grace" to music. In the 1930s, Hubert was the music director for noted evangelist Paul Rader. One day in a pastor's office Hubert saw the words of this poem on a plaque, and, personally moved, he composed a wonderful melody for them and turned the popular poem into a beloved hymn.

Hubert Mitchell didn't just put "He Giveth More Grace" to music; he put the words into practice. If God's multiplied peace can sustain us at home, Mitchell pondered, why not overseas? Why not wherever God takes us?

Feeling God's call to Indonesia, Hubert and his wife, Helen, traveled to the island of Sumatra in 1935 to share the message of God's peace, and they had some astonishing adventures. On one occasion, for example, Hubert and his coworkers plunged into the island's interior to search for the elusive Kubus, a tribe of aborigines. It was a rigorous trip through thick and dangerous jungles, but one evening they broke into a clearing and found a Kubu settlement.

The village women and children ran away, having never before seen a white man. The warriors surrounded the missionaries with spears and poison-tipped blowguns. But when the missionaries explained their purpose, the

Kubus welcomed them warmly and Hubert was taken to the chief's hut to spend the night.

The next morning, the village assembled to hear what Hubert had to say. The missionary opened his Indonesian Bible to John 19 and began to read about the death of Christ. He explained who Jesus was, and slowly went through the story of the Lord's crucifixion. At one point, the chief raised his hand and asked, "What is a cross?"

Hubert went to the edge of the clearing, cut down two large saplings, stripped off their branches, and lashed them together to form a cross. He placed the cross on the ground and laid down on it, stretching his arms along the beam.

"But how could a man die, lying there upon two trunks of trees?" asked the chief.

"He was crucified," said Hubert. "They drove sharp nails into His hands and feet."

"What is a nail?" asked the chief.

Hubert struggled to describe a nail. He ransacked his duffle bag looking for anything resembling a nail, but came up empty. He could see the villagers losing interest in the story, and some began drifting away. It was time for lunch, so the meeting broke up and Hubert went down to the stream and prayed, saying, "Please, Lord, give me some way to explain a nail to these people."

Someone handed him a banana leaf, filled with rice and dried fish, and afterward Hubert reached into his knapsack and took out a can of mandarin oranges for dessert. The oranges, which Hubert purchased in a Chinese store near his home base, had been canned in Japan. Opening the oranges, he poured them into a dish and was about to throw away the can when he heard a rattling sound. There, to his amazement, was a shiny new three-inch nail. It had been hermetically sealed in the can, perfectly preserved with the oranges.

"Look!" he shouted. "This is a nail! This is what they used to nail Jesus to the cross." The chief ran over and took the nail from Hubert's hand. He felt its sharp point against his palm. As the tribe reassembled, Hubert continued the story of Jesus, His death and resurrection, and the people were totally absorbed by the message. They began crying, "How great the love of God! How great the love of God!" One by one, the members of the Kubu tribe confessed Christ as Savior and were baptized in the nearby stream. These new believers began going to other tribes with the same message, and in this way the gospel spread through central Sumatra.

According to Hubert Mitchell's niece, Karen, who attends our church in Nashville, his story was one of sacrifice and stress, but he lived out the concept of multiplied peace. The Lord imparted grace to him, giving it over and over and over again. To multiplied trials, God multiplied peace.[4]

I love the premise of "more grace" and "multiplied

peace," because that's what I so badly need. The God of miracles, who can drop nails into cans of sliced oranges, can hammer His peace into our hearts. He doesn't just *add* peace to our lives, but He drives it in, nailing it down, magnifying it, multiplying it. The Bible's answer to anxiety and worry is spelled p-e-a-c-e.

THE PEACE OF GOD

In Philippians 4, the Lord presents this to us in two ways: in verse 7, we read about the *peace of God*, and in verse 9, we encounter the *God of peace*.

In verse 7, God makes a pledge to us. When we consciously and actively incorporate the habits we've been talking about throughout this book, those habits will produce a reality in our lives that no amount of money can purchase; something that has eluded the presidents, prime ministers, and premiers of history. We will become recipients of something so powerful and pervasive it will forever change our lives, our personalities, our anxiety levels, our legacies—everything about us: "The peace of God, which transcends all understanding, will guard your hearts and your minds in Christ Jesus."

This kind of peace is God's kind of peace, His own unlimited measure of composure—strong, deep, fathomless, unshakable, impregnable, and grounded in eternal hope. It is the serenity of the Trinity—derived from the

Father, purchased for us by the Son, installed in our hearts and instilled within our minds by the Holy Spirit.

God never feels a worried moment. He dwells above all the cares of the world, inhabiting eternity and occupying infinity. He knows the end from the beginning. No threat can disturb Him and no foe can threaten Him, for He—He alone—is the Creator, Sustainer, and Commander of the universe and all it contains. He is the Ruler of all reality, in all realms, in all epochs and ages, whether seen or unseen, whether visible or invisible. His infinite power merges with limitless love to reassure His people of His obstinate providence. He can replace your transient worries with transcendent peace.

Because God is infinite, His measureless peace is never exhausted, nor even diminished, regardless of its outflow.

Because He is unchanging, His peace is unwavering.

Because He is almighty, His peace is all-powerful, fully able to pull down the strongholds of anxiety in our lives.

Because He is omnipresent, His peace is available to every one of us, everywhere, on every occasion, in every location, wherever we find ourselves.

Because He is all-knowing, His peace is astute, perceptive, and unerring.

Because God is faithful, His peace is steadfast.

Philippians 4:7 goes on to describe the peace of God as being a peace *"which transcends all understanding."* In other words, the peace of God defies all attempts to describe, analyze, explain, or comprehend it. This is the peace that God Himself possesses within the infinity of His attributes. It's the peace that flows from Him like currents in the ocean and streams in the desert, and it is transcendent. The word used here means "to surpass, to transcend, to exceed, to go beyond, to rise above, to be overarching, and to arc around."

Let's use all these synonyms and create our own expanded paraphrase of the verse: "The peace of God, which surpasses, exceeds, transcends, goes beyond, rises above, and arcs around all human understanding—that is the peace that will guard your hearts and minds."

In Ephesians 3:19, Paul used similar terminology about the love of God, when he wrote that God's love "surpasses knowledge." Just think! In Philippians 4:7, we have the peace of God that transcends understanding; in Ephesians 3:19, we have the love of God that surpasses knowledge. What multiplied gifts from Him who gives more grace!

The next phrase in the verse tells us what this incredible peace does for us: "The peace of God, which transcends all understanding, *will guard . . .*" The word in the original Greek is a military term for a contingent of solders assigned to protect someone. It implies having a bodyguard or a protective force around you. Security services speak of creating bubbles or perimeters around their clients, and if the client is a head of state, there may be concentric protective perimeters around them wherever they go.

The peace of God isn't just a warm feeling of wellbeing or an ephemeral emotion. It's as tough as a soldier, as tenacious as a marine, as stalwart as a seaman, as adamant as an airman. It's God's Special Forces, arrayed like a bodyguard stationed at the entrance of your thoughts and your emotions—your heart and your mind—to protect and keep you.

Notice how both heart and mind are mentioned: "The peace of God, which transcends all understanding, will guard *your hearts and your minds.*"

When it comes to worry and anxiety, there is both a mental and an emotional aspect to them. It's impossible to chart the border between our thoughts and feelings, for they are intertwined like threads in embroidery. But we know from experience how our minds and our hearts bear our concerns differently. Sometimes I have more trouble with an anxious mind when my problems barge in and commandeer my thoughts. On other occasions, my nerves are edgy, and I experience feelings of uneasiness, even when my mind struggles to pinpoint the source. My thoughts give me headaches, and my feelings give me stomachaches.

That's why the God of peace sends two detachments of soldiers to help—one to compose our minds with truth and the other to guard our emotions with trust. As

J. B. Phillips translates it: "The peace of God which transcends human understanding, will keep constant guard over your hearts and minds as they rest in Christ Jesus" (PHILLIPS).

Philippians 4:7 has its roots in Isaiah 26:3–4, which says, "You will keep in perfect peace those whose minds are steadfast, because they trust in you. Trust in the LORD forever, for the LORD, the LORD himself, is the Rock eternal."

Notice the parallels between Isaiah 26:3–4 and Philippians 4:7. God Himself is our source of peace, and the peace is indescribable—a perfect peace, a peace that transcends human understanding. Likewise, in Isaiah 26, the word *keep* conveys the idea of a military guard stationed around the steadfast mind, the mind that is stayed on Jehovah and founded on an unshakable Rock.

Isaiah later compared the peace of God to a river flowing through the soul (Isaiah 66:12), and hymnist Frances Havergal combined the pictures to give us a visual portrait of God's peace:

> *Like a river glorious is God's perfect peace,*
> *Over all victorious, in its bright increase;*
> *Perfect, yet it floweth, fuller ever day,*
> *Perfect, yet it growth, deeper all the way.*
> *Stayed upon Jehovah, hearts are fully blest,*
> *Finding, as He promised, perfect peace and rest.*[5]

I especially love Havergal's second verse, which says when we're hidden in God's perfect hand, no foe can follow and no traitor stand:

> *Not a surge of worry, not a shade of care,*
> *Not a blast of hurry touch the spirit there.*[6]

That brings us to the last phrase of Philippians 4:7: God's peace will guard your hearts and minds "*in Christ Jesus.*" When you study this subject of peace throughout the Bible, the most consistent fact is its connection with Jesus Christ. Years ago, this was popularized on church signs by the slogan: "Know Christ, Know Peace. No Christ, No Peace." Perhaps the phrasing is trite, but the truth is inescapable when one studies the subject of peace in the Scriptures.

- In Isaiah 9:6, the Messiah is called the "Prince of Peace."
- In Isaiah 53:5, we read, "He was pierced for our transgressions, he was crushed for our iniquities; the punishment that brought us peace was on him."
- When Jesus was born in Bethlehem, the angels proclaimed "peace on earth" (Luke 2:14).
- The book of Acts says the message of the gospel is "the good news of peace through Jesus Christ" (Acts 10:36).

- Romans 5:1 says, "Therefore, since we have been justified through faith, we have peace with God through our Lord Jesus Christ."
- Ephesians 2:14 says, "For he himself is our peace."

Additionally, Jesus said in John 14:27, "Peace I leave with you; my peace I give you. I do not give to you as the world gives. Do not let your hearts be troubled and do not be afraid." Those were among Christ's final words as He met with His disciples in the Upper Room on the eve of His crucifixion. He gave them His last will and testament.

How many times have we watched television shows in which families gather for the reading of someone's last will? We wait in suspense to see who will be millionaires and who will be paupers. In John 14:27, Jesus issued His will. He didn't have property or houses to leave; He didn't even have a pillow for His head. He didn't have money; Judas Iscariot had absconded with our Lord's last shekel. He couldn't leave His clothing; His executioners would divide that among themselves. But He did have one thing to leave His disciples—His perfect, transcendent, unassailable peace.

How tragic when we fail to claim our inheritance! When we live in anxiety and frantic worry even though Jesus Christ, in the last hours of His life, bestowed on us the legacy of His own peace. Nothing could be more beneficial to your heart and mind than to memorize

John 14:27. Learn this verse well and ponder it often, so that the Holy Spirit can bring these word to your mind and apply them to your heart during the rough patches of life.

I had a friend in college named Scott Burlingame. He married a wonderful woman named Joyce, and they devoted their lives to ministry. While Scott was serving as a pastor in Columbia, South Carolina, he was diagnosed with cancer, and the news went from bad to worse. Scott's illness proved terminal. During their months on this journey, Joyce sent prayer updates to friends, and these updates read like journal entries. After Scott's death, she compiled them in a book entitled *Living with Death, Dying with Life*. One of her entries was dated January 17:

> These are truly hard days. Although Scott can eat just a little, it is not much. I am carefully trying to add new foods, but then find we are back where we started. And drinking enough liquids is also a problem . . . even water is difficult. A mixture of water and Gatorade seems to work the best. He is very weak, and I have to assist him in much of what we took for granted just a few months ago.
>
> I have had to buy him all new clothes twice. . . . The hospice people came yesterday for an initial visit. . . . Right now things are very difficult. I feel as though the hosts of hell have been unleashed against us to bring worry, frustration, confusion, and to attempt to make us doubt all

we believe. But, in the words of an old song, "Christ has regarded our helpless estate, and has shed his own blood for our souls!" And in Him we live and move and have our being, and are able to withstand the onslaught of the enemy. Underneath the anguish is the deep peace of God that passes all understanding.[7]

God's peace isn't the absence of conflict or the non-existence of problems. It is the Gulf Stream of His grace below the surface levels of life. We lay hold of the transcendent peace of the God of peace, which can stabilize our thoughts and emotions in every situation. That's God's ironclad promise to those who will take refuge in Him.

THE GOD OF PEACE

But the Lord doesn't stop with that. Philippians 4:9 brings another promise to us—one that's even greater than the promise of God's peace: *"The God of peace will be with you."*

The only thing better than the *peace of God* is the *God of peace*, who promises to be with us forever. Imagine! Having the peace of God within you, and the God of peace beside you.

Throughout the Bible, we see God portrayed as the ever-present God of peace. There's an interesting story in the book of Judges, for example. When the Lord appeared to Gideon to commission him for His work, Gideon was alarmed. He realized he had seen the angel of God, which was tantamount to seeing God Himself, and he was agitated. He expected to die. But the Lord spoke to him aloud, saying, "Peace! Do not be afraid. You are not going to die" (6:23). Judges 6:24 says, "So Gideon built an altar to the LORD there and called it The LORD Is Peace."

A more literal translation of this is "Jehovah-Shalom," or "Yahweh-Shalom," and it's one of the great biblical names for God: The Lord Is Peace.

The priestly benediction in Numbers 6 says, "The LORD turn his face toward you and give you peace" (v. 26). Similar is the benediction at the end of 2 Thessalonians: "Now may the Lord of peace himself give you peace at all times and in every way. The Lord be with all of you" (3:16).

Likewise, 1 Thessalonians 5:23 says, "May God himself, the God of peace, sanctify you through and through." If the God of peace is sanctifying us through and through, growing us, developing us, and making us more spiritual and more holy, it only makes sense that we would experience more of His peace throughout the process.

I've quoted a lot of verses in this chapter, and when we pull them all together, we have a stockpile of Scripture reinforcing these twin truths about the peace of God and the God of peace. Let's review them once more, and you might circle the one that speaks most to you as you read them. Doing so will help you begin developing the habit of peace today:

- "Thou wilt keep him in perfect peace, whose mind is stayed on thee: because he trusteth in Thee. Trust ye in the LORD forever; for in the LORD JEHOVAH is everlasting strength."
- He called the altar Jehovah-Shalom—the Lord is peace.
- "Peace I leave with you; My peace I give you. I do not give you as the world gives. Do not let your hearts be troubled and do not be afraid."
- "Since we have been justified through faith, we have peace with God through our Lord Jesus Christ."
- "He was pierced for our transgressions, He was crushed for our iniquities; the punishment that brought us peace was on Him."
- "He Himself is our peace."
- "I have told you these things, so that in Me you may have peace. In this world you will have trouble. But take heart! I have overcome the world."
- "Great peace have those who love Your law, and nothing can make them stumble."
- "May God himself, the God of peace, sanctify you through and through."
- "Now may the Lord of peace himself give you peace at all times and in every way."

Grow familiar with these verses and remind yourself

of them if you feel guilty whenever a ray of peace shines through your heart and dispels a cloud of anxiety. Sometimes I think to myself, *If I have peace of mind, I must be out of my mind. I have a responsibility to worry; and how can I, in good conscience, go around without, as Havergal put it, a surge of worry, a shade of care, or a blast of hurry? I need the adrenaline of anxiety to solve this crisis.*

Biblical peace isn't a lighthearted, devil-may-care attitude of frivolity. It takes life seriously, and it's aware of the gravity of any situation. But when peace rules in the heart, the soul is anchored in the storms. It isn't the adrenaline of anxiety we need, but the Prince of Peace. Peace and strength are siblings; they are twins. Psalm 29:11 says, "The LORD gives strength to his people; the LORD blesses his people with peace."

Notice the words "his people." Our peace depends on a relationship with God through Jesus Christ. The most important phrase in Philippians 4:7 is at the end of the verse: "in Christ Jesus." This was Paul's signature line. In reading through his letters in the New Testament, we see this phrase again and again—in Christ, in Christ, in Christ! All our blessings are in Him. All our hope is in Him. All our peace is in Him, and He is our very life.

I recently had the opportunity to speak at a Christian gathering in Interlaken, Switzerland. After the second or third night, I noticed an elderly woman on the second row listening intently throughout my message. The next

night I went up and spoke to her. Shortly afterward someone asked me, "Do you know who that was—the woman
to whom you were speaking?"

"No, I don't."

My friend said, "That woman is the last surviving
member of Winston Churchill's secret corps of spies."

During World War II, Churchill bypassed the British
intelligence service, MI6, and he secretly recruited an
army of spies who operated directly under his authority.
They were primarily saboteurs. Few people in the government knew of their existence, though at its zenith, there
were about thirteen thousand people involved. This nest of
spies was headquartered in a building on Baker Street, and
they sometimes were called the Baker Street Irregulars.

This woman—Noreen Riols—was the last of them.

The next night after the service I asked if I could talk
with her. She was very friendly and willing to talk. She
told me that for sixty years following the war, she had
not been allowed to tell anyone what she had done. The
British government kept the existence of Churchill's Secret
Army a classified secret until the year 2000. Even her own
mother didn't know the truth of it, but had always thought
Noreen had worked for the Ministry of Agriculture and
Fish during the war.

When the official records were unsealed in 2000,
Noreen could finally talk about her experiences. She was
only a teenager when recruited, and she worked on British

soil, training and helping support the saboteurs. She fell in love with one of the secret agents. "He was a very brave man," she said. "He was going on a last dangerous mission and they said, 'Only he can do it. If anyone can pull it off, he can.' But he was too well-known. He should never have gone. He promised me that this was his last mission, really his last. But he didn't come back."

All she had of him was a picture, which she kept in the back of her billfold until it was stolen; then she had nothing of him.

When the war ended, she said, it was difficult trying to return to normal. She was now unemployed and unable to tell anyone what she had done. It was a rough transition, and as time went by she tumbled into depression. At the age of forty, she had an abortion, which, she said, did her in. "I fell into a terrible, terrible depression. I was twice in a psychiatric hospital and was about to go in for the third time. But I said, 'No, no, I'm not going back.' Some dear friends came and said, 'Look, these medications are not helping, and you are taking more and more of them.'"

Noreen's friends started praying earnestly for her, and she agreed to let them pray for her. But there followed what she called "terrible months of miseries and grayness and blackness . . . I came to the end of myself; and when you come to the end of yourself there really isn't anywhere else to go, is there? I was suicidal, by the way. It was awful."

But then, through the witness of her friends, she came

to the knowledge of the Lord and found Jesus Christ as her Savior. That's when everything changed. "He gave me peace, which is something I hadn't had for a long time," she said, "and then gradually life became beautiful again."[8] For many years, she has faithfully attended Bible conferences and grown in her love for Scripture and the peace it brings her through Christ. That's why she had come to Interlaken, and that's how I met her.

Jesus summed up all this in John 16:33: "I have told you these things, so that in me you may have peace. In this world you will have trouble. But take heart! I have overcome the world." And—one more verse—Psalm 119:165 says, "Great peace have those who love your law, and nothing can make them stumble."

This is the normal Christian experience: guarded around the clock by the peace of God and walking every moment with the God of peace.

I don't want to dissuade you from seeking medical help or quality counseling as you deal with the difficult issues of life. As I said at the beginning of this book, many gifted people can help us with our struggles in life, and I thank God for skilled professionals who come alongside us with their support, therapy, medical skill, and psychological resources. Yet we know the best help in the world will be tremendously enhanced by the truths of Scripture, but diminished without the dogged practice of the habits called for in its pages.

You've been worried long enough. Let the Lord Jesus Christ have complete control over your life and over all your problems and concerns, every one of them. Rejoice in Him. Be gentle. Don't be anxious about anything but pray about everything. Find things for which to be thankful. Meditate on God's Word. Learn from others and follow the example of those who trust Him fully.

Gradually life will become beautiful again, the peace of God will guard your thoughts and emotions—a peace that transcends all understanding. Marvelous peace. Perfect peace. Multiplied peace. For the Lord gives strength to His people; He blesses His people with peace.

Additional Resources

nxiety is something that you will live with. One book isn't going to give you all of the answers you need. I've compiled some additional resources to help you along your journey.

PODCAST SERIES: WHATEVER HAPPENS . . .

Whatever Happens is a podcast series on the Robert J. Morgan podcast that takes the listener through the entire book of Philippians. The series starts with episode 112. Scan the QR code and start listening.

GOD WORKS ALL THINGS TOGETHER FOR YOUR GOOD

We all need more confidence and joy. Romans 8:28 is a remarkably powerful verse. "We know that all things work together for the good of those who love God." *God Works All Things Together for Your Good* not only empowers us to deal effectively with everyday stress and strain, but offers solid assurance to anyone facing serious trouble. Morgan

shares strong techniques for reversing misfortunes, finding purpose in painful situations, and turning discouragement into resilience. This book, video study, and study guide will help live a more confident and joy-filled life.

THE INVISIBLE THREAD

Few people in this world have ever reached out and felt that invisible thread, but it's there for every one of us. It is the perfect will of God. For every one of us, there is an invisible thread to guide us through our lives. God has an individual plan for each person who is committed to Jesus Christ as Lord and Savior.

Scan the QR code to learn more about the invisible thread and how through everything Lord Jesus Christ will lead us to where He wants us to be and bless us in doing what He wants to do.

SPIRITUAL DEPRESSION

The book that has been the most helpful to me in dealing with issues of anxiety is *Spiritual Depression: It's Causes and It's Cure* by D. Martyn Lloyd-Jones.

Available wherever books are sold.

Notes

A WORD FROM THE AUTHOR:

1. https://www.who.int/news/item/02–03–2022-covid-19-
   pandemic-triggers-25-increase-in-prevalence-of-anxiety-
   and-depression-worldwide

2. Amy Spencer, "Amanda Seyfriend: The Most Down-To-
   Earth member of the Glam New Guard," *Glamour*, www.
   glamour.com/magazine/2010/03/amanda-seyfried-the-most-
   down-to-earth-member-of-the-glam-new-guard.

3. I came across this quotation long ago but do not know its
   original source; one option is the mystery novelist Arthur
   Somers Roche.

4. George Müller, *The Autobiography of George Müller* (New
   Kensington, PA: Whitaker House, 1984), 155.

5. Gretchen Rubin, *Better Than Before: What I Learned About
   Making and Breaking Habits* (New York: Broadway Books,
   2015), Kindle location 70.

6. Ibid., Kindle location 215.

CHAPTER 1

1. The other Old Testament usages of "Rejoice in the LORD" can be found in Psalms 64:10; 97:12; and 104:33–34; Isaiah 29:19 and 41:16; and Joel 2:23.

2. Phyllis Thompson, *Count It All Joy* (Wheaton, IL: Harold Shaw Publishers, 1978), 13.

3. Ibid., 14.

4. Ibid., back cover.

5. Joy Ridderhof, *Are You Rejoicing?* (Los Angeles, CA: Global Recordings Network, 1984), entry for day 1.

6. https://hymnary.org/text/ rejoice_the_lord_is_king_your_lord_and_k

7. Katie Hoffman, *A Life of Joy* (n.p.: Ano Klesis Publishing, 2006), 150–51.

8. QUERY: Endnote was empty but reference still in text. Pls confirm deletion is intentional.

CHAPTER 2

1. Murat Halstead, *The Illustrious Life of William McKinley: Our Martyred President* (n.p.: Murat Halstead, 1901), 422.

2. James Ford Rhodes, *The McKinley and Roosevelt Administrations, 1897–1909* (New York: The Macmillan Company, 1922), 107. Not all scholars accept the historical accuracy of this story.

3. Adapted from numerous newspaper articles, including "Fliers' Prayers Answered," www.nzherald.co.nz/nz/ news/article.cfm?c_id=1&objectid=10511547; and "Pilot of Doomed Aircraft Claims That His Passenger's Prayers Helped the Pair Land Safely," www.dailymail.co.uk/news/

article-1020917/Pilot-doomed-aircraft-claims-passengers-
prayers-helped-pair-land-safely.html; and other similar
articles.

4. Personal conversation with Dr. Don Wyrtzen and based
   on notes for his class on Worship and Prayer, delivered at
   Liberty University on October 8, 2015.

5. Michele Robbins, *Lessons from My Parents: 100 Moments
   That Changed Our Lives* (Sanger, CA: Familius, 2013), 4–5.

6. Ibid.

7. This account is based on numerous media stories, including
   James P. Moore, "American Prayers, On D-Day and Today,"
   Washington Post, June 6, 2004, B03. Also see *The American
   Legion Magazine*, vol. 116–17, p. 81. Mark Batterson also
   researched this story and shared it in his book *ID: The True
   You* (Maitland, FL: Xulon Press, 2004), 88–89.

8. The original copy of this speech is displayed at the Franklin
   D. Roosevelt Presidential Library and Museum in Hyde
   Park, New York.

9. Cameron V. Thompson, *Master Secrets of Prayer* (Madison,
   GA: Light for Living Publications, 1990), 65.

10. Charles A. Tindley, "Leave It There," hymn published in
    1916.

11. The Theosophical Society in America, *The Theosophical
    Quarterly*, 25 (1927), 185. I also relate this story in my
    devotional book, *All to Jesus.*

12. Ibid.

CHAPTER 3

1. This story appeared in numerous newspapers in September 1981, including *Gaffney Ledger*, September 4, 1981; *Schenectady Gazette*, September 4, 1981; *Daytona Beach Morning Journal*, September 4, 1981; and in Steve Petrone, "Woman, 85, Proves She's Tough-As-Nails After Her 4 Days in Horror Swamp," *Weekly World News*, September 29, 1981.

2. Ibid., 141, 183–84.

3. A. W. Tozer, *The Knowledge of the Holy* (New York: Harper & Row Publishers, 1961), 83.

4. William M. Anderson, *The Faith That Satisfies* (New York: Loizeaux Brothers, 1948), 165.

5. Maxwell Cornelius, "Sometime We'll Understand," hymn published in 1891.

CHAPTER 4

1. Daniel Haun, "2013: What Should We Be Worried About? Global Cooperation Is Failing and We Don't Know Why," *Edge*, https://www.edge.org/response-detail/23773.

2. Peter Schwartz, "2013: What Should We Be Worried About? A World of Cascading Crises," *Edge*, https://www.edge.org/response-detail/23881.

3. Ibid.

4. Debbye Turner Bell, *Courageous Faith: A Lifelong Pursuit of Faith Over Fear* (Grand Rapids: Discovery House, 2021), 90–92.

5. Ibid., 25.

6. Albert Mohler, "Thanksgiving as a Theological

Act," November 23, 2016, AlbertMohler.com, http://www.albertmohler.com/2016/11/23/ thanksgiving-theological-act-mean-give-thanks/.

7. Quoted by Sally Clarkson and Sarah Clarkson in *The Lifegiving Home* (Carol Stream, IL: Tyndale House, 2016), 213.

8. Robert A. Emmons, *Thanks! How Practicing Gratitude Can Make You Happier* (Boston: Houghton Mifflin Company, 2007), 11.

9. Ibid., 22.

10. Ibid., 3.

11. Ibid., 11.

12. Janice Kaplan, *The Gratitude Diaries: How a Year Looking on the Bright Side Can Transform Your Life* (New York: Dutton, 2015), Kindle location 183.

13. Ibid., Kindle location 148.

14. Ibid., Kindle location 188–89.

15. Martin Rinkart, "Now Thank We All Our God," 1636, translated into English by Catherine Winkworth.

16. Linda Derby, *Life's Sticky Wick*, privately published manuscript, 2010. Used by permission.

17. Ibid.

18. Carmel Hagan, "The Secret to an Efficient Team? Gratitude," *99U.com*, http://99u.com/articles/37261/ the-secret-to-an-efficient-team-gratitude.

19. E. A. Johnston, *J. Sidlow Baxter: A Heart Awake* (Grand Rapids: Baker Publishing Group, 2005), 124–26.

20. Ibid.

21. Ibid.

22. Ibid.

CHAPTER 5

1. Arthur L. Young, "Attitude and Altitude," *New Outlook: Volume 8, Number 11*, November, 1955, 42.
2. James Allen, *As a Man Thinketh* (New York: Barnes & Noble Books, 2002), 3, 22, 25.
3. Ibid., 43.
4. Quoted in J. I. Packer, *Knowing God* (Downers Grove: InterVaristy Press, 1973), 13.
5. Some of this material is adapted from my book *Reclaiming the Lost Art of Biblical Meditation* (Nashville: HarperCollins, 2016), where the reader can find these ideas expanded into a variety of practical applications.
6. Geoffrey T. Bull, *When Iron Gates Yield* (Chicago: Moody Press), passim.
7. These insights came from attending an Institute of Basic Youth Conflicts seminar in the 1970s.
8. As told to Dr. Gary Mathena, director of practica for the School of Music at Liberty University, by his father, Dr. Harold Mathena.

CHAPTER 6

1. *The Obstinate Horse and Other Stories from the China Inland Mission* (Shoals, IN: Kingsley Press, 2012), chapter 1.
2. Ibid.
3. Mary K. Crawford, *The Shantung Revival* (The Revival Library, www.revival-library.org), and Dennis Balcombe,

China's Opening Door (Lake Mary, FL: Charisma House, 2014), 27.

4. William Wilberforce, *The Correspondence of William Wilberforce, Volume 1* (London: John Murray, 1840), 131–33.
5. Ibid.
6. "The Wisdom of Love" by Ian Maclaren, in *The Advance*, March 8, 1906, 298–99. This story is likely a fictional work by Maclaren, but it may well have been a fictionalized account of the experience of the Scottish pastor John Watson, who was best known by his pen name—Ian Maclaren. In other words, the story of John Carmichael seems to have been a fictionalized autobiography.
7. You can watch and listen to these lectures at buckhatchlibrary.com—and you'll be glad you did!
8. Bill Bright, *Revival Fires* (Orlando, FL: New Life Publications, 1995), 83–84.

CHAPTER 7

1. Monica Cantilero, "Married for 75 Years Without a Single Fight," Christian Today, August 11, 2015, www.christiantoday.com/article/married.for.75.years.without.a.single.fight.us.christian.couple.gets.medias.attention/61583.htm.
2. Jessica Bringe, "Area Couple Celebrates 75 Years of Marriage," *WEAU News*, www.weau.com/home/headlines/Area-couple-celebrates-75-years-of-marriage-320981951.html.
3. Fred Smith, Sr., *Breakfast with Fred* (Ventura, CA: Regal, 2007), 48–49.

4. Helen Steiner Rice, *Poems of Faith* (Carmel, NY: Guideposts, 1981), 33–34.

5. Donna Kincheloe, *I Never Walk the Halls Alone* (Nashville, TN: ACW Press, 2007), 72–74.

6. Ibid.

7. Based on a conversation with Rocky Forshey; used with permission.

8. John Wooden, *The Essential Wooden* (New York: McGraw-Hill, 2007), 8–9.

9. Ibid.

10. Ibid., 11.

11. Quoted by Harold C. Lyon in *Tenderness Is Strength: From Machismo to Manhood* (New York: Harper & Row, 1977), 7.

CHAPTER 8

1. Thomas Watson, *A Body of Practical Divinity* (Philadelphia: James Kay), 224.

2. Charles Haddon Spurgeon, *The Metropolitan Tabernacle Pulpit: Sermons Preached and Revised By C. H. Spurgeon During the Year 1890: Volume 36* (London: Passmore & Alabaster, u.d.), 421 and 430.

3. Annie Johnson Flint, "He Giveth More Grace," copyright 1941, renewed 1969 by Lillenas Publishing Company.

4. Based on conversations with Karen Singer and adapted from Hubert Mitchell, *The Story of a Nail* (Santa Clara, CA: Westmar Printing, Inc., 1978).

5. Frances Ridley Havergal, "Like a River Glorious," 1876.

6. Ibid.

7. Joyce Burlingame, *Living with Death, Dying with Life* (Bloomington, IN: Westbow, 2015), 130–31.

8. Based on a personal interview.

About the Author

Robert J. Morgan is a Bible teacher who travels extensively for speaking engagements, seeking to deepen the shallowing church and strengthen the growing church in America and beyond. For over forty years, he was a pastor in Nashville, Tennessee. He is a best-selling, gold-Illuminations, and gold medallion–winning writer with more than thirty-five books in print and over five million copies in circulation in multiple languages. Rob has appeared on numerous television and radio shows. He speaks widely at churches, conferences, schools, and corporate events.

Rob is also a homemaker and was a caregiver for his late wife of forty-three years, Katrina, who battled multiple sclerosis and passed away in November of 2019. He and Katrina have three daughters, sixteen grandchildren, and four great-grandchildren.

He is also the host of The Robert J. Morgan podcast, in which he teaches through books of the Bible expositionally.

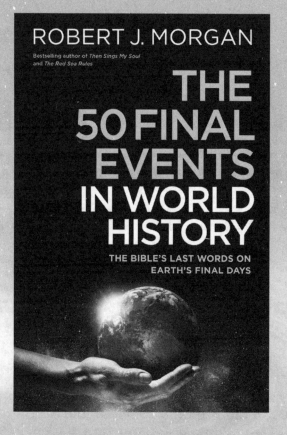